Orkney by Air

A photographic journey through time

by

Guy Warner

kea publishing

First published in 2005 by
kea publishing
14 Flures Crescent
Erskine
Renfrewshire PA8 7DJ
Scotland

Copyright © Guy Warner, 2005

British Library Cataloguing in Publication Data

Guy Warner
Orkney by Air
1.Aeronautics, Commercial – Scotland – Orkney – History
2.Aeronautics, Commercial – Scotland – Orkney – History – Pictorial works
I.Title
387.7'0941132

ISBN-10: 0951895877

Cover: Jane Glue's rendition of Highland Airways GA Monospar, G-ACEW,
over St Magnus Cathedral and the Kirkwall Hotel.

Printed in Scotland by Iain M. Crosbie Printers, Beechfield Road, Willowyard
Industrial Estate, Beith, Ayrshire KA15 1LN

Contents

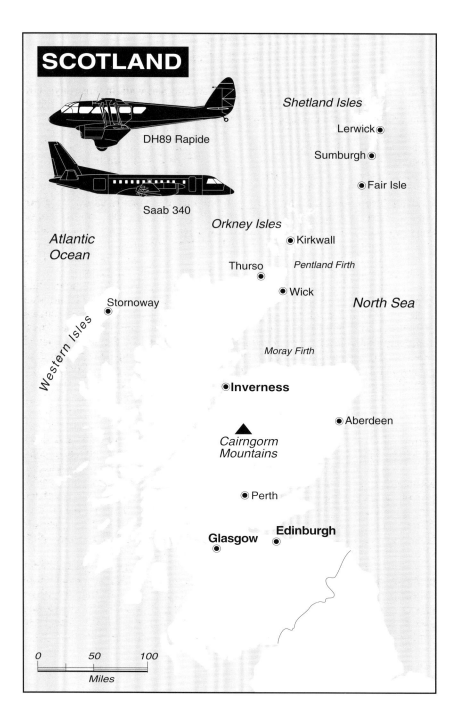

SCOTLAND

DH89 Rapide

Saab 340

Atlantic
Ocean

Western Isles

Shetland Isles

Lerwick⊙

Sumburgh⊙

⊙Fair Isle

Orkney Isles

⊙Kirkwall

Thurso
⊙

Pentland Firth

⊙Wick

North Sea

Stornoway
⊙

Moray Firth

⊙Inverness

▲
Cairngorm
Mountains

⊙Aberdeen

⊙Perth

Glasgow
⊙

Edinburgh
⊙

0   50   100

Miles

Foreword
by Scott Grier OBE, Chairman of Loganair

It is almost exactly thirty years since I first flew into Kirkwall. In those days, UK aviation was strictly regulated, and Loganair was restricted to the minor services while British Airways, having recently emerged from British European Airways, was responsible for air services on the main routes in Scotland. To make my journey to Kirkwall, I had travelled with my wife and infant twin sons from Ayrshire to Edinburgh Turnhouse Airport for the Loganair flight to Inverness Dalcross on a Britten-Norman Trislander. After a scheduled wait of several hours at Dalcross, we flew north by BN2 Islander to Wick and then on, eventually, to Kirkwall. The boredom of this long journey was undoubtedly eased when my wife, on checking in for the Islander flight at Dalcross, was required to be weighed - much to the intense curiosity of our fellow passengers. A very public embarrassment was avoided by my quick-thinking wife grabbing a twin under each arm before stepping on to the scales. Fortunately, flying has come a long way since then, but that first flight to Orkney remains a vivid memory.

I was excited at the prospect of visiting Orkney for the first time. I had seen any number of photographs of Loganair Islanders flying past the Old Man of Hoy, when the pilot clearly had chosen the "scenic route" with his passengers enjoyment more on his mind than the profits of his employer! I also knew something of Orkney's rich archaeological heritage and of the strategic naval importance of Scapa Flow in both World Wars. Despite having been prepared for Orkney in this way, I still was immediately enchanted by the place. My empathy with all things Orkney has not diminished with the passage of time.

Since the early days, Orkney has been very aviation conscious – in my view probably even more than the Western Isles or Shetland. Of course, Orkney benefited hugely from Captain Ted Fresson's pioneering work in the 1930s. His sterling efforts to establish air services from Inverness to Orkney and other islands, and from Kirkwall to some of Orkney's North Isles were almost straight out of *The Boy's Own Paper*. Orcadians took quickly to flying, and aviation became a great influence on their way of life. Air services became an essential part of the transportation system within the islands and this was encapsulated very graphically by the late Councillor Jack Scott in his book, *Wings over Westray*. Loganair's contribution, too, has been considerable, ever since the Company acquired a Britten-Norman Islander aircraft in 1967 to re-establish some of the inter-island services flown by Fresson before the War.

With Orkney having such a long and varied history of flying, *Orkney by Air* needed to be written. Guy Warner's book makes fascinating reading as it traces its 'aviation journey through time' and captures the importance of air services to Orkney and its people. The many photographs he has acquired, and used to illustrate his book, have brought this aviation history to life. Many will read *Orkney by Air* with keen interest tinged with more than a little nostalgia.

Scott Grier
West Kilbride, Ayrshire July 2005

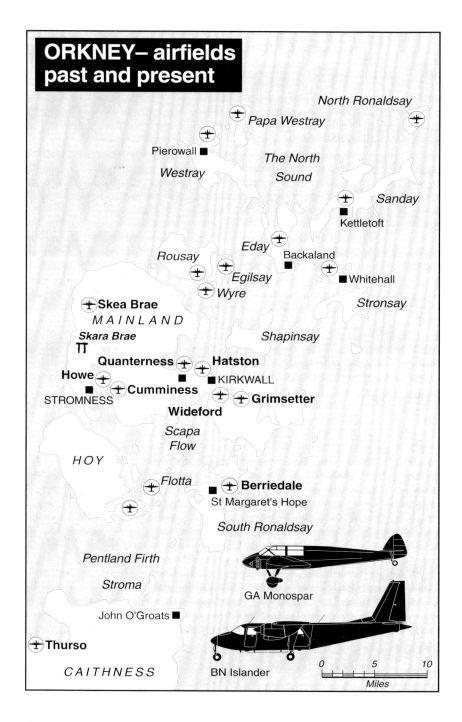

ORKNEY– airfields past and present

North Ronaldsay

Papa Westray

Pierowall ■

Westray

The North
Sound

Sanday

Kettletoft ■

Eday

Backaland

Rousay

Egilsay

Whitehall ■

Wyre

Stronsay

Skea Brae

MAINLAND

Skara Brae
ᴨ

Shapinsay

Quanterness

Hatston

Howe

KIRKWALL

Cumminess

STROMNESS

Grimsetter

Wideford

Scapa
Flow

HOY

Flotta

Berriedale

■ St Margaret's Hope

South Ronaldsay

Pentland Firth

Stroma

GA Monospar

John O'Groats ■

Thurso

CAITHNESS

BN Islander

| 0 | | 5 | | 10 |

Miles

4

Introduction

Some sixty-seven islands and islets make up the Orkney archipelago, seventeen of which are inhabited by people as well as a profusion of seabirds and seals. The human population, which numbers approximately 19,000, is concentrated on the largest island, known as the Mainland, on which are located the two largest towns, Kirkwall and Stromness.

The landscape was fashioned by the glacial erosion of the underlying sandstone, limestone and igneous rocks, creating low, undulating hills, covered by fertile glacial drift deposits. Orkney has no mountains, the highest ground rising to just over 500 metres on the island of Hoy, which literally means 'High Island' from the Old Norse 'Haey'.

The prevailing westerlies sweeping across the Atlantic Ocean have resulted in a climate that has its fair share of wind and rain, though the effect of the Gulf Stream means that frost and snow are rare. The weather can change both frequently and dramatically - it is said that all four seasons may be experienced in a single day or less. The horizon appears limitless and sunsets can be spectacular. The air is both pure and clear.

Visitors remark upon the scarcity of trees, the length of the days in summer (over eighteen hours in June), and the spectacular views from sea-cliffs sculpted by marine erosion. The scenery is truly beautiful, and includes farms, moorland, lochs and trout streams. The sea and the sky are ever-changing shades of blue and grey, while the land is picked out in pastel shades of purple, brown and green.

Orkney is one of Scotland's richest farming counties. Beef cattle, sheep, fish farming, lobsters and salmon are all important to the local economy.

The islands are known to have been inhabited from prehistoric times, the underground Neolithic village of Skara Brae, which dates from about 3200 BC, being a fine example of early man's skill and industry. A Roman fleet under Agricola is known to have visited the islands in 78 AD. Norse raiders stayed longer, colonising Orkney by the end of the 9th century and beginning a period of rule as a Viking earldom under the Norwegian crown, which lasted until 1231 when control passed to the Scottish Earls of Angus. In 1472, in compensation for the non-payment of Margaret of Denmark's dowry, it became part of the Scottish kingdom of James III. Christianity had come to the islands in the early medieval period. The first recorded missionary visit was by Cormac in 580. St Boniface Kirk on Papay is believed to occupy a site dating from the 8th century, Earl Sigurd was converted in 995, Christ's Kirk on West Mainland was founded in 1057, and in 1137 St Magnus Cathedral was founded in Kirkwall.

The southernmost tip of Orkney is only six and a half miles from John O'Groats, but the sea passage is across the often stormy and hazardous waters of the Pentland Firth. Here the Atlantic Ocean rushes to meet the North Sea and experienced boatmen say there are ten tides. In the years following World War One, this stretch of water provided both a challenge and an opportunity. It became apparent that the air routes within the British Isles that were most likely to succeed were those which required a sea crossing, where aerial navigation was quicker and more direct. Orkney provided the additional factors of wind, rain, fog and storm. For the challenge to be met successfully, the requirements were reliable aircraft that could carry a profitable load and pioneers of vision, ambition, bravery and perseverance. *Orkney by Air* highlights the endeavours of these men and women.

Few lives in Orkney are unaffected by air transport. In common with the rest of the United Kingdom, aircraft bring in mail, newspapers, freight, tourists and businessmen; and depart with both local produce and Orcadians visiting Scotland and beyond. However, Orkney's relationship with the aeroplane is special - it is a lifeline for many, a matter of life or death for some, a provider of essential services – not least of all for hospital patients and visitors to mainland hospitals - and a major factor in the re-generation of the communities living on the outlying islands of the group.

A touch of winter at Kirkwall Airport, c. 1980 (Michael Firth)

Fresson's first flights

The story begins in April 1931 when Captain Ernest Edmund Fresson and his passenger, Miss Helen Pauer, flew to Kirkwall in the de Havilland DH60G Gipsy Moth, G-AAWO, landing in a field near the Balfour Hospital on the Scapa Pier road just by the town boundary. His purpose was to seek out a suitable landing ground for the operation of public 'joy-riding' flights in the summer. Ted Fresson had worked in the tea trade in China before World War One. He learned to fly in Canada and the USA before seeing active service in England flying anti-submarine patrols. He returned to China after the war where he gave flying instruction and was involved in aircraft construction. He came back to England in 1928 and spent several seasons giving 'joy rides' to the public all round Britain. He is regarded as the father of civil aviation in Orkney.

On 22 August 1931, Captain Fresson returned in the Avro 504K, G-EBGZ, of the North British Aviation Company, landing some three miles from Kirkwall in a field near the Deerness Road. He made the flight from Wick carrying two passengers, the 'boots' from the Station Hotel and a friend. Fresson was pleased by the interest shown by the owner of *The Orcadian*, James Mackintosh. Fresson later recorded: "[Mackintosh] became dedicated to my later efforts in establishing airline connections to the south. His columns were always at my disposal no matter how many I required."

In early September, Fresson commenced "joy-riding" from a field belonging to Hatston Farm. He also flew several trans-Pentland charters, including the 18-year-old Miss Agnes Shearer, a reporter for *The Orcadian*, who became the first Orkney resident to fly over the Firth to Wick.

Captain Fresson returned to Orkney in G-AAWO, accompanied again by Helen Pauer, in February 1932. He landed in a field adjacent to Peedie Sea, a large pool on the west side of Kirkwall, and as the weather promised to be stormy overnight, the aircraft was towed into town and accommodated in a shed owned by the coal merchant J G Shearer. After seeking backing from many quarters, Fresson achieved a degree of financial security by the award of a contract to carry *The Scotsman* newspaper by air from Inverness to Kirkwall. He also had the possibility of a Royal Mail contract if he could maintain regular operations for a year.

Highland Airways Ltd was registered in Edinburgh on 3 April 1933, to operate air services in Northern Scotland, with an initial capital of £2,625. The Managing Director and Chief Pilot was, of course, Ted Fresson.

Ted Fresson with his Avro 504K, 1931. (Courtesy of Orkney Library - Photographic Archive (OLPA))

Joy-riding passengers awaiting the arrival of Fresson's Avro 504K, 1931. (OLPA)

Point Field, Trimland Farm, Rousay, where Fresson was offering joy rides in his de Havilland DH60G, G-AAWO, at five shillings a time. (OLPA)

Wings folded, Fresson escorts G-AAWO to undercover storage in Kirkwall during his 1932 visit. (OLPA via Robert Foden)

G-AAWO is eased into Shearer the coal merchant's shed. The Chinese characters correspond to the aircraft's registration 'Aa-wo'. (OLPA)

Highland Airways'
Monospar, G-ACEW
Inverness, *on North*
Ronaldsay. (OLPA)

North Ronaldsay
passengers are
greeted by Fresson
from the wing of the
Monospar. (OLPA)

DH83 Fox Moth G-
ACCT of Midland &
Scottish Air Ferries
was loaned to
Fresson in July 1933
following an accident
with the Monospar at
Wideford. (OLPA)

The first scheduled services

On 8 May 1933 the inaugural service of Ted Fresson's Highland Airways to Kirkwall from Inverness via Wick was flown in General Aircraft Monospar ST4, G-ACEW, *Inverness*. The aircraft "presented the appearance of a silver bullet crossing the sky," according to *The Orcadian*. The journey time was one hour and thirty minutes (including fifteen minutes on the ground at Wick), the fare was £3, and three passengers plus a consignment of The *Scotsman* were carried. The landing was made at Wideford Farm, a couple of miles south of Kirkwall, some thirty acres of which Fresson had leased for a five year term. He later wrote, "They [the Orcadians] took to the air like ducks to water. Also, they turned out to be very loyal to Highland Airways in the competition we had to combat later on."

Three days later, on 11 May, a service from Kirkwall to Thurso was begun by Highland Airways. This was given up after a time as Ted Fresson was not happy with the airfield near Thurso. Disaster struck the fledgling company on 3 July 1933 when G-ACEW crashed on approach to Wideford. There were no casualties, but the aeroplane was badly damaged. How could Fresson maintain the service and win the vital Post Office contract? Owing to the generous spirit of John Sword, another great pioneer of Scottish aviation, all was not lost. He assisted Fresson in his time of need by providing aircraft from his Renfrew-based company, Midland & Scottish Air Ferries. These were DH83 Fox Moth, G-ACCT, and the Airspeed AS.4 Ferry, G-ACBT. After a fortnight Ted Fresson was able to return to 'normal' service with a leased Monospar, G-ABVN. He also tested the DH84 Dragon I demonstrator, G-ACCE, on the route.

On 2 August 1933, Highland Airways began flying services with a new DH84 Dragon I, G-ACIT. Fresson was very impressed by his latest acquisition: "It was an easy and delightful aeroplane to fly and had a remarkable take-off with a full load which fitted in very well with our small airfields." This elegant biplane, constructed of spruce, plywood and fabric, first flew in November 1932. It was cheap to operate and simple to maintain. In the words of the noted aviation historian, John Stroud, the Dragon had "a major role in the development of British domestic air services." A hangar was erected at Wideford and a base engineer, Cyril Pugh, established on site.

Highland Airways' de Havilland Dragon, G-ACIT, on North Ronaldsay. (OLPA)

Novelist Eric Linklater (1899-1974) (second right) is among those greeting a passenger from G-ACIT, now carrying the titles of Scottish Airways. (OLPA)

Air letters, and Aberdeen

On 7 May 1934 a new service was inaugurated by Highland Airways with the first flight from Aberdeen to Kirkwall via Wick in the DH84 Dragon I, G-ACIT, named *Aberdeen*. At Aberdeen, a landing site at Seaton, on the coast close to the golf links, was used.

A very important development was the award of the first UK internal Royal Mail airmail service pennant to Highland Airways. The airmail route, Inverness to Kirkwall, was flown by Ted Fresson in DH84 Dragon I, G-ACCE, on 29 May 1934. He wrote, "It was a red letter day for me, as it meant I had conquered all that I had set out to do in those early days when I was hunting around Kirkwall for capital to finance the company. We had now obtained the four essentials I had been looking for, finance, passengers, mail and newspapers." To mark the occasion, pleasure flights were offered from Wideford "for short flights at 5/- (25p) and 7/6 (37p) per head, and for tours incorporating Finstown 10/- (50p), Stronsay 15/- (75p) Sanday £1." A celebration luncheon was held at the Kirkwall Hotel.

The commencement of on-demand services to the North Isles came on 6 August 1934. (On 3 October 1933, flying the Moth, G-AAWO, with Thurso businessman, Peter Angus, as his passenger, Fresson had alighted on the island of Sanday in a field adjacent to the Kettletoft Hotel. Later this would become the landing ground for services to the island. They were en-route to Lerwick in Shetland, but had to break their journey on Sanday because of bad weather.)

Airstrips were laid out on Stronsay, Sanday, Hoy (Longhope), Rousay, Westray and North Ronaldsay. The single fare from Kirkwall to Rousay was 7/6, and to North Ronaldsay it was 15/-. Ted Fresson had toured the islands in July in Monospar *Inverness* giving 'joy rides' to the islanders to drum up interest and to test the market. He observed: "Undoubtedly the outstanding air–conscious island was North Ronaldsay. The islanders converted two fields, uneven of surface, into a twenty-eight acre airfield, flat, free from obstacles, the finest in all the North Isles - made in a day!" The farmers on all the islands gave the landing facilities free.

Later in the month, on 29 August, Highland Airways suffered a setback when the DH84 Dragon I, G-ACCE, hit a stone wall when taking off from Kirkwall. The pilot and passengers were not badly hurt, but the aircraft was written off.

A contract was awarded to Highland Airways in October by the Orkney County Council to operate an air ambulance service to convey patients between the North Isles and the Balfour Hospital in Kirkwall. Later it was extended to carry urgent cases from Orkney to Aberdeen. November saw the first use of more advanced eight-passenger DH89 Dragon Rapides. Fresson borrowed G-ACPO, one of the early production models, for a few days and was much

The official welcoming party waiting at Wideford for the first Airmail to arrive in Orkney without surcharge. (OLPA)

INAUGURATION

OF THE

ORKNEY AIR MAIL

COMMEMORATIVE LUNCHEON

AT THE

KIRKWALL HOTEL, KIRKWALL
TUESDAY, MAY 29, 1934

*Under the Patronage of the Provost,
Magistrates and Councillors of
the City and Royal
Burgh of Kirkwall*

Menu cover for the Orkney Air Mail commemorative luncheon. (OLPA)

Newspapers being delivered by air, collected by Peter Murray and Peter Cursiter. (OLPA)

G-ACCE, Caithness, the de Havilland Dragon I that flew the inaugural air mail service on 29 May 1934. (OLPA)

De Havilland Dragon II, G-ADCT, Orcadian, on Westray. (OLPA)

impressed by this enhanced development of the DH84, which was faster than the Dragon, had a greater load carrying ability, and had a better reserve of power in case of trouble. Its higher approach speed did mean that it needed a longer landing distance, so rather than lengthen his airfields, Fresson suggested to de Havilland that flaps could be fitted to the wings. This proposal was incorporated and, by April 1935, a modified aircraft was ready for testing.

Partners and Rivals

As the land at Seaton had been reserved for the Highland Show, in May 1935 Highland Airways moved its Aberdeen base to a new airfield at Kintore, which is on the road to Inverurie. At about this time discussions were held in Glasgow with a view to a merger with United Airways of Blackpool, which was backed by the wealthy Whitehall Securities Group. These talks were successful with Highland Airways retaining its own identity, but gaining greater financial security. It also brought Ted Fresson into a working agreement with Northern & Scottish Airways of Renfrew, which was run by another major figure in Scottish aviation history, George Nicholson.

27 May 1935 saw the start of competition from E L Gandar Dower's Aberdeen Airways service from Aberdeen to Stromness. Eric Leslie Gandar Dower was a tough and unyielding character, but possessed of great charm. He was regarded by Ted Fresson as an interloper in what became quite a bitter battle for customers. Gandar Dower's pilots included two great pioneers of Scottish aviation, Eric Starling and Henry Vallance. Aberdeen Airways used the airport that he was developing at Dyce, and, in Orkney, an airfield at Howe, a farm two miles outside Stromness on the main road to Kirkwall, was established. The nearby Cumminess airstrip was also used for a time. The principal aircraft was the DH84 Dragon I, G-ACAN.

Aberdeen Airways' Short S.16 Scion, G-ACUV, on South Ronaldsay. (OLPA)

Aberdeen Airways' next move was to begin flying to Stromness from Thurso, using Clarendon Aerodrome, which was to the east of the town. The inaugural service was on 11 June 1935.

On 6 September 1935 a violent downdraught caused the DH84 Dragon II, G-ADCT, *Orcadian*, of Highland Airways to crash into trees at Westerness on Rousay. The pilot and five passengers escaped without injury. The aircraft was dismantled, taken by rowing boat to Kirkwall, and repaired. It was flying again by November.

Aberdeen to Orkney flights by Aberdeen Airways were suspended for the winter on 3 December, but an aircraft was based at Thurso for services to Stromness, with an on-demand stop available at Berridale near St. Margaret's Hope on South Ronaldsay. This was before the construction of the causeway linking South Ronaldsay to the Mainland. Later Longhope on Hoy was added to the on-demand service.

Dragon G-ADCT is being disassembled at it is extracted from the vegetable garden of Westerness House, Rousay, following its accident on 6 September 1935. (OLPA)

Aberdeen Airways also served South Ronaldsay with de Havilland Dragons. G-ADFI, The Silver Ghost, is seen here taxying on South Ronaldsay's airfield. (OLPA)

Brig o' Waithe, Stenness, was the site of the pre-WWII airfield for Stromness. (Robert Foden)

17

Aberdeen Airways' Dragon G-ADFI prior to departure from Cumminess to Thurso during the summer of 1936. (OLPA)

Highland Airways' hangar at Kintore nears completion at its Aberdeen base in 1935. The aircraft is de Havilland Rapide G-ACPN. (courtesy of Philip Jarrett)

Services to Shetland

At the start of 1936, Aberdeen Airways began using another landing ground at Quanterness, just to the west of Kirkwall. And, on 2 February, Eric Starling flew Aberdeen Airways' first air ambulance flight in the DH84 Dragon II, G-ADFI, taking a patient from South Ronaldsay to Stromness for transfer by road to the Balfour Hospital. Starling wrote in his log: "Owing to the strong wind, I took Mr Williams and Alf Cormack with me to give a hand on the ground." The helpers' role was to grab hold of the wingtips and keep the aircraft from blowing over once it had come to a halt. This was a common technique for the aviation pioneers on Orkney in those days.

The first service from Aberdeen (Dyce) to Shetland (Sumburgh) by Aberdeen Airways was flown non-stop by Eric Starling in the DH89, G-ADDE, on 2 June. The service was subsequently flown via Thurso and Stromness or Quanterness, normally with a DH84. The following day, Fresson began services from Aberdeen (Kintore) to Sumburgh via Orkney with the DH89, G-ACPN, of Highland Airways. This was the company's first Dragon Rapide. G-ACPN was obtained on a lease and was delivered on 19 April 1936 still in British Airways' livery.

Fresson felt somewhat aggrieved, as Highland Airways' service was a long-planned development whilst Aberdeen Airways' inauguration the previous day was arguably a slightly devious publicity stunt. Highland Airways in due course also published an 'Official Guide'. This well-illustrated booklet featured a foreword from Ted Fresson, a brief history of Highland Airways, a guide on what the passenger would view from the air flying north from Inverness or Aberdeen, indexes of services to Kirkwall and Sumburgh, and descriptive essays for the visitor. In his introduction, Fresson referred to Highland Airways as "the pioneers of air travel in the north ....and still leading." This may well have been an indication of his opinion of the competition at this time.

Highland Airways promotional brochure. (OLPA)

De Havilland Dragon II, G-ACNJ, of Allied Airways (Gander Dower) Ltd. (OLPA)

Two Orphir girls (and a violin) board Allied Airways' Dragon I, G-ACLE, at the end of school holidays. (OLPA)

Amalgamation, and a babe in arms

Aberdeen Airways changed its name to Allied Airways (Gandar Dower) Ltd. on 13 February 1937. On 1 August 1937, Scottish Airways was created by the merger of Highland Airways (which had previously merged with United Airways) with Northern & Scottish Airways, which was part of the same group, controlled by Whitehall Securities. The Northern and Southern divisions of Scottish Airways continued to operate with a considerable degree of autonomy, but it was a mixed blessing for Fresson. While it gave much greater financial backing, he lost some of his independence of action.

Meanwhile, on 15 April, several newspapers reported that Allied Airways had carried its youngest passenger, Lesley McLetchie, who was just five weeks old and was born in an Aberdeen nursing home. She flew from Aberdeen to Kirkwall with her mother and father, Dr and Mrs J L McLetchie. It was reported that, "the hum of the engines appeared to have a soothing effect on her, for she slept most of the way."

A Glasgow (Renfrew)-Perth-Inverness-Kirkwall-Sumburgh service was inaugurated on 2 May 1938 by the DH89, G-AFEY, of Scottish Airways flown by David Barclay.

In the autumn of 1938, Captain John Hankins was installed at Tankerness House as the Scottish Airways base manager. Located in Broad Street, Kirkwall, opposite the cathedral, Tankerness House exists today as one of Scotland's finest sixteenth-century town houses and the home of the Orkney Museum.

Tankerness House, Kirkwall. (Author)

Regulation, and a red letter day for North Ronaldsay

In 1939, the UK Government decided that all scheduled air services should be licensed. Among the licensed routes approved by the Government's newly created Air Transport Licensing Authority in February were the following:

Allied Airways (Gandar Dower) Ltd

Thurso - South Ronaldsay - Stromness

Aberdeen - Wick - Thurso - Kirkwall

Aberdeen - Thurso - South Ronaldsay - Kirkwall

Kirkwall - Shetland

Scottish Airways

Kirkwall - Sanday - Stronsay - Westray - Longhope - North Ronaldsay

Kirkwall - Wick

Inverness - Wick - Thurso - Kirkwall

Kirkwall - Shetland

Thurso - Longhope - Kirkwall

In all, forty-seven routes stretching from Shetland to the Channel Islands were licensed to fourteen companies.

At the end of February, a very hazardous air ambulance mission was carried out by Scottish Airways' pilot John Hankins. He landed on Sanday in dark and stormy conditions, with the landing strip illuminated only by the headlights of two strategically positioned cars to form a letter 'L' on the grass. Ted Fresson wrote: "This flight I consider was the highlight of all our urgent ambulance flights and I have always admired the skill and courage of Captain Hankins in undertaking that call."

In the summer of 1939, a new service was planned by Scottish Airways linking Orkney to London in six hours. It would depart from Kirkwall at 6.25 am, connecting with the Airspeed Envoys of North Eastern Airways at Perth and so to Croydon via Edinburgh and Newcastle. The outbreak of war only a few months later prevented this service operating long enough to enable its viability to be assessed.

A significant development took place on 31 July 1939 when the first regular airmail service from Kirkwall to North Ronaldsay was flown by Ted Fresson in the Scottish Airways DH84 Dragon I, G-ACIT, now named *Orcadian* and based in Kirkwall for the inter-island services. (This aircraft is now Britain's oldest surviving airliner and may be seen at the Science Museum, Wroughton, Wiltshire.)

On 31 August 1939, the final pre-war Kirkwall-Thurso service was flown by Henry Vallance of Scottish Airways. On 3 September 1939 the inter-island services were suspended due to the outbreak of war. They were resumed in November, but finished again on 27 April 1940. The landing grounds were blocked by the building of stone cairns. Stromness and Thurso aerodromes were later taken over by the military and permanently immobilised.

Captain Ted Fresson (in overalls) delivering the mail to North Ronaldsay in DH84 Dragon I, G-ACIT, July 1939. (OLPA)

Another mail delivery to North Ronaldsay. Dr Garvie (far right) looks on. (OLPA)

Background: De Havilland Dragons and a Rapide at Wideford. (Courtesy of Peter V Clegg)

World War Two

Initially, all Orkney air services were suspended with the declaration of war. Fresson was soon given the task of providing charter flights to perform vital military communications links for the government to Orkney and Shetland. In the first instance he had only one aeroplane, the DH89 Dragon Rapide, G-ADAJ. As it soon became obvious that a regular air service was needed for personnel, dispatches and spares, Fresson was instructed to resume a schedule as soon as possible. During the war Scottish Airways served Inverness-Kirkwall-Sumburgh (and briefly Wick as well). Allied Airways (Gandar Dower) Ltd flew Aberdeen-Wick-Kirkwall-Sumburgh. The aircraft were camouflaged with earth and green colouring, which had the effect of merging the topsides with the peat and heather surroundings. At Kirkwall, both airlines used Wideford (as Gandar Dower had closed Quanterness). On 18 March 1940, DH89A Dragon Rapide, G-AFEY, of Scottish Airways crashed at Wideford. Soon afterwards RNAS Hatston became operational and both Fresson and Gandar Dower were given permission to use that airfield instead.

However, in late 1941, DH89 Dragon Rapide, G-ACZF, of Allied Airways crashed into a stone wall when landing, again at Wideford. It was dismantled and sent back to Dyce by sea. Operations moved to RAF Skea Brae for a time in 1941, and then to RAF Grimsetter in 1942. Grimsetter is located approximately one mile to the east of Wideford Farm and is still in use as Kirkwall Airport. On 10 December 1941, DH89, G-ADAJ, of Scottish Airways was the first aircraft to land at RAF Grimsetter.

Thousands of passengers, and tons of freight and mail were carried. Servicemen and women were taken to and from leave. Morale was maintained by the speedy delivery of parcels, letters and newspapers. Essential spare parts, and couriers with important messages, were carried. Air ambulance work was an important task. Refugees who had escaped from Norway in small boats were flown south. Searches were made for torpedoed ships and for survivors on life rafts. Enemy aircraft were encountered and evaded.

When asked about the contribution made by Allied Airways to the war effort, Eric Gandar Dower replied: "Were we helped? No. The RAF wanted everything. Our staff were constantly called up and we struggled on, using more and more 'string', giving the best service we could. The 15-hour day became 16 or even 18! No ranks, no gongs, no uniform, no recognition! The Hun was a bare half-hour away. Defenceless, we passed them in the air!"

A service was also operated by 1680 Communications Flight between Abbotsinch, and later Prestwick, to the Western Isles, Orkney and Shetland. The de Havilland Dominie X7372 (the military version of the Rapide) was used for almost five years from August 1941. The original pilot was Flight Lieutenant John Hankins AFC, who had extensive pre-war experience with Scottish

Airways and was regarded as one of the finest pilots in the airline. Some commanding officers insisted that the men should take their military duties very seriously and insisted on regular firearms practice. One crew member fulfilled this command by borrowing a shotgun to stalk rabbits on Sanday.

This four-engine DH86 Express, L8040, in service as a transport with 782 Naval Air Squadron, suffered an undercarriage collapse at Hatston on 22 January 1944 while being marshalled in bad weather conditions. (OLPA)

Passengers, bound for the Kirkwall market, board Scottish Airways DH89A Rapide, G-AGJG. The windows of the aircraft are masked for WWII service and the aircraft carries pseudo military identification. (OLPA)

Allied Airways' timetable for 1940. (Courtesy of Philip Jarrett)

Opposite: Rapide, G-ACZE, of Scottish Airways following an aborted take-off from Grimsetter, 27 December 1945. (OLPA)

Scottish Airways' 1944 schedule. (OLPA)

Hatston becomes Kirkwall's airport by the sea

In 1945, Allied Airways (Gandar Dower) Ltd services flew from Aberdeen to Wick, Kirkwall and Lerwick. Scottish Airways flew connections from Glasgow through Inverness to Wick, Kirkwall and Shetland. Both companies used DH89 Dragon Rapides. Hatston was again used as the civil airfield for Kirkwall during this period. Back in January 1939, Ted Fresson had been asked by the Admiralty to advise on a suitable site for a Naval Air Station in Orkney. He recommended Hatston. He stated that tarmac runways should be laid rather than grass strips, which somewhat surprised the naval experts. He explained: "After five difficult winters at Wideford airfield, struggling to take-off with heavy loads in a sea of mud, I am convinced that the Navy will never get away with a standard grass airfield in Orkney." Later, he wrote: "As far as I am aware that was the first airfield constructed in the British Isles which was provided with hard strips for take-off and landing. When it was completed Hatston airfield caused some concentrated thinking in the RAF, for many senior officers arrived in Kirkwall to inspect the finished job. Within a couple of years, the hard strip became the standard practice for the wartime airfields built all over the country."

On 27 June 1945, Ted Fresson flew Major Nevin Spence MP in the DH84 Dragon I, G-ACIT, on an electioneering campaign around the islands, landing on Stronsay, Sanday, Eday, Westray, Papa Westray and North Ronaldsay. He later took the Orkney Council Road Surveyor, John Robertson, to make a survey of the airfields on North Ronaldsay, Sanday, Stronsay and Westray. The year ended less happily when, on 27 December 1945, DH89, G-ACZE, crashed and suffered considerable damage after engine failure on take-off from RAF Grimsetter.

Kirkwall town showing the location of Hatston. (OLPA via Robert Foden)

Fresson's resilient Dragon I, G-ACIT, at Hatston in 1947. (OLPA via Robert Foden)

Opposite: Ted Fresson with his son, Richard, and a taste of the future at Kirkwall, a Douglas DC-3 of British European Airways. (OLPA)

The end of the independent airlines

The Orcadian questioned the benefits that would accrue to Orkney in the event of the nationalisation of air services with the election of the Labour Government in 1945. Would a board sitting in London, or even the Scottish Advisory Committee in Edinburgh, give sufficient consideration to Orkney's particular reliance on civil air transport? The record of Scottish Airways was praised and Orcadians were hailed as the most air-minded people in the British Isles. Meanwhile, on 22 August 1946, DC-3 G-AGZA of Railway Air Services was brought to Kirkwall by Ted Fresson to make trial landings at Hatston and some two dozen Orkney citizens were given the experience of flying in a large, modern aeroplane. "The electric lights in the cabin were switched on and one could read, in comfort, a fine selection of picture and general magazines and that morning's Sunday newspapers," enthused *The Orcadian*'s reporter. The pilots were Captain Bill Baillie and Captain Donald Prentice.

Sadly, time was running out for the pioneers. The nationalisation of Scottish Airways by British European Airways (BEA) became effective on 1 February 1947. Ted Fresson did not find life comfortable within the rules and restrictions imposed by the management of the state corporation. It can be argued with some justification that he was very shabbily treated.

Allied Airways was brought into the state-owned BEA on 12 April 1947. Two days later, in an astonishingly insensitive move, the BEA management told Ted Fresson to travel over to Aberdeen to effect the take-over. Fresson later wrote: "I have always felt that at that moment Gandar Dower and I became friends in adversity. We had been blatantly robbed of many years' hard work and effort."

Worse was to follow when, on 11 February 1948, Ted Fresson, who had been appointed BEA manager for the Highlands and Islands, flew a charter in DH84 Dragon I, G-ACIT, to Westray with three inspectors from the Ministry of Civil Aviation. While there, he received an urgent request to uplift a seriously injured boy from Stronsay and take him to the Balfour Hospital. He was severely rebuked by senior management for carrying out this mercy mission without full prior authority. Within a fortnight he was made redundant and he left the company on 31 March. The famous Orcadian writer, Eric Linklater, commented: "He endeared himself to the islanders because he was not only a brilliant pilot and a business-like manager but a humane and charitable person who would always undertake a hazardous flight, if called upon. Captain Fresson has been deprived of his livelihood and his life's work; the north of Scotland has been deprived of a public servant of outstanding worth and ability." Fresson spent the early 1950s flying in East Africa, but passed his final years back at Inverness.

Ted Fresson's final tour of the islands in 1948 with Gerry Meyer, editor of The Orcadian. *The aircraft is, of course, G-ACIT,* Orcadian. *(OLPA)*

Douglas DC-3, G-AGZA, of Railways Air Services, seen here undergoing maintenance at Renfrew, made trial landings at Kirkwall in 1946. (Courtesy of Richard Riding)

A venture in air cargo delivery

1948 saw the beginning of a short-lived experiment in the delivery of lobsters, fresh eggs and other perishable goods to London by air. The aircraft used was a Miles Aerovan 4, G-AJZP, of Air Cargo Distributors and flown by Miles' test pilot, Ulsterman, Eric Esler. Miles also investigated and came up with a proposal for an air ambulance service using a twin-engine Miles Gemini. Several Geminis, including G-AKKE, G-AIDO and G-AKEH, visited Orkney. A third Miles type, the unique M.71 Merchantman, G-AILJ, flown by the Company's Chief Test Pilot, Ken Waller, delivered a Hillman Minx from Reading to Kirkwall in June for Mr John Nicholson, at a cost of £35.

Another positive development came in June 1948 when Captain David Barclay, the manager of BEA's Air Ambulance Unit, flew DH84 Dragon I, G-ACIT, to evaluate landing grounds on Stronsay, Sanday, North Ronaldsay, and Westray.

Miles Gemini, G-AKKE, was mooted as an air ambulance aircraft. (Courtesy of Peter Amos)

Miles Merchantman G-AILJ's sole commercial service was to deliver this Hillman Minx to John Nicolson (second left) in Kirkwall. (J W Sinclair / Norman Sinclair)

The early BEA Years

Over the course of thirty-seven years, BEA served and developed the routes connecting Kirkwall to Aberdeen, Inverness, Wick, Sumburgh, Edinburgh and Glasgow. The aircraft used during the first fifteen years were as follows:

DH89 Dragon Rapide 1947-1952

This grand old type flew on and on, providing island services for BEA as the *Islander* class. It served Tiree and Barra, as well as being used for ambulance flights, until 1955. In BEA service, it continued on the Lands End to Isles of Scilly route until its retiral in 1964.

However, the Rapide's post-war career with BEA in Orkney was short. On 15 January 1949, DH89 Dragon Rapide, G-AHXV, on an air ambulance flight, tipped over and was severely damaged while landing on water-logged grass on North Ronaldsay. It was declared a write-off and BEA became ever more reluctant to send aircraft to the smaller airstrips. This incident may well have killed off whatever slim chance there had been at that time of reviving air services to the North Isles. Despite petitions and entreaties from the islanders, BEA did not feel that there was sufficient prospect of a profitable service. In February 1950, for the first time in British election history, ballot boxes were delivered by air in a specially chartered BEA Rapide from Shetland for the count in Kirkwall, at a cost of £50. The newly elected MP was Jo Grimond, who became leader of the Liberal Party in 1956

BEA intended to replace all its Rapides with Handley Page Marathons in 1951, but, in the event, the order was cancelled as it was decided that the aircraft was unsuited to the role. Another potential replacement type was the DHA-3 Drover, but this was not pursued either. The last service made by the Rapide from Kirkwall for BEA was on Tuesday 30 September 1952 by G-AGSK.

Former Highland Airways and Scottish Airways de Havilland Rapide, G-ADAJ, in service with BEA at Aberdeen.
(Aeroplane / www.aeroplanemonthly.com)

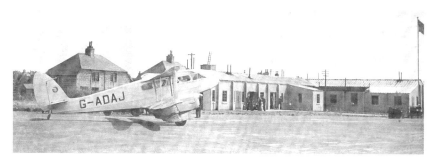

Junkers JU52/3m 1947

These fourteen-seat aircraft were wholly unsuitable for air services around the Scottish islands. They had been seized from Germany as war reparations and converted for civilian use by Shorts of Belfast. As they had been constructed to wartime specifications, they were much less reliable than pre-war JU52s, as the Germans, not unreasonably, anticipated that they would have a relatively brief working life. BEA called it the *Jupiter* Class, but they were expensive and uneconomic to operate, and also required a small mobile power plant to start up the motors. *The Orcadian* greeted their arrival with the headline, "Ex-Enemy Planes Now Welcome." The most serious incident to occur happened on a flight from Kirkwall to Aberdeen when the crew were almost asphyxiated by carbon monoxide gas from one of the engines, which penetrated the cockpit. The pilots sealed off the passenger cabin and opened all the cockpit windows. They tried shutting down one engine at a time to find the source of the lethal fumes. By the time they had done so and had isolated the problem, they were very drowsy indeed. It was not long before the *Jupiters* were withdrawn.

Junkers JU52/3m during refurbishment in Belfast for entry to BEA service, September 1946. (Short Brothers Ltd / Bombardier Aerospace Belfast)

Douglas DC-3 Dakota/Pionair 1947-1962

This long-serving type was subsequently named the *Pionair* class in 1950 following conversion by Scottish Aviation at Prestwick to 32-passenger configuration and with the addition of built-in airstairs. It was powered by twin Pratt & Whitney Wasp radial piston engines and cruised at 180 mph.

Return fares and flying times from Kirkwall in the late 1940s and early 1950s were as follows: London - 4 hours 54 minutes, £24 (via Edinburgh and Aberdeen); Shetland - 45 minutes, £5 3s (£5.15); Wick - 25 minutes, £2 8s (£2.40); Inverness - 1 hour, £5 4s (£5.20); Aberdeen - 1 hour 20 minutes, £5.18s (£5.90).

Passengers board a BEA Douglas DC-3 at Grimsetter, c. 1950.
(OLPA)

takes you there

Grimsetter Airport, Orkney to :—

London. Weekday service at 4.40 p.m. Flying time :
4 hrs. 54 minutes. Return Fare : £24.0.0

Shetland. Weekday services at 10.25 a.m., 2.40 p.m.
and 4.35 p.m. Flying time : 45 minutes.
Return Fare : £5.3.0

Wick. Weekday service at 1.0 p.m.
Flying time : 25 minutes.
Return Fare : £2.8.0

Inverness. Weekday services at 10.15 a.m., 1.0 p.m.,
5.0 p.m. Flying time : 1 hour.
Return Fare : £5.4.0

Aberdeen. Weekday services at 9.35 a.m., 2.0 p.m.,
4.40 p.m., 5.20 p.m. Flying time : 1 hour 20 mins.
Return Fare : £5.18.0

**Reservations: Principal Travel Agents (no booking fee) or
B.E.A., 7 Broad Street, Kirkwall.   Tel.: Kirkwall 159**

and brings you back

BRITISH   EUROPEAN   AIRWAYS

*BEA
advertisement
for services from
Kirkwall, 1948.*

35

Some 1950s visitors to Kirkwall

In the mid-1950s, many interesting aircraft visited Kirkwall, none more so than those featured on this page. The DH114 Heron 1B, G-ANXA, of BEA had just entered service for Air Ambulance duties in 1955. The visit of the Westland S51 Dragonfly, G-ANAL, in the same year, was sponsored by the *Scottish Sunday Express* and was the first civil helicopter to visit Orkney. The BEA Viscount V701, G-AMOH, arrived in 1956 on a proving flight, although scheduled services with this type would not begin for another six years. A Westland Whirlwind brought the Queen Mother on an official visit in August 1956.

BEA de Havilland Heron 1B, G-ANXA, at Kirkwall in 1955. (OLPA via Robert Foden)

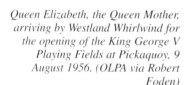

Queen Elizabeth, the Queen Mother, arriving by Westland Whirlwind for the opening of the King George V Playing Fields at Pickaquoy, 9 August 1956. (OLPA via Robert Foden)

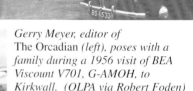

Gerry Meyer, editor of The Orcadian *(left), poses with a family during a 1956 visit of BEA Viscount V701, G-AMOH, to Kirkwall. (OLPA via Robert Foden)*

The first civil helicopter to visit Orkney, Westland S51 Dragonfly, G-ANAL, August 1954. (OLPA via Robert Foden)

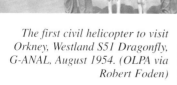

The Viking Connection

Faroe Airways operated scheduled services with Douglas DC-3s during the period 1963-1965 from Copenhagen to Vagar via Kirkwall. This was due to the enterprise of local businessmen John McDonald and Charlie Flett, and also because Sumburgh, the other likely transit point, did not have Avgas that the Dakota required for refuelling. In the early 1970s, the Danish airline, Danair, operating Fokker F27s, ran a similar schedule once a week for a couple of years.

1974/75 Danair timetable, Copenhagen-Kirkwall-Vagar. (Courtesy of Björn Larsson)

Faroe Airways Douglas DC-3, OY-DMN. (Photo and Faroese DC-3 and Fokker Friendship aviation stamps courtesy of Anker Eli Petersen)

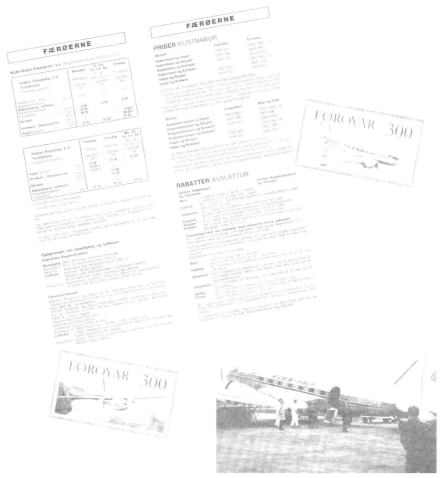

The later BEA years
Handley Page Herald 1962-1966

The Herald was a high-wing, twin-engine aircraft, powered by Rolls-Royce Dart turboprops. It had accommodation for forty-eight passengers. Three of this type, G-APWB, G-APWC and G-APWD, were used by BEA, all leased from the Ministry of Supply. The first commercial service by a Herald in Scotland was by G-APWB on 16 April 1962 when it flew from Glasgow to Sumburgh via Aberdeen, Wick and Kirkwall. The Herald was seemingly well suited to island operations, having a low slung fuselage giving ease of loading as well as a large freight door, but it did not prove economical to operate on the Scottish routes. The small size of the fleet also had the effect of increasing the related spares, maintenance and crew training costs.

A contemporary Handley Page house journal featured an article on the Herald in Scotland. It noted that BEA's Highlands and Islands services were run at a loss 'largely as a social service', but highlighted their vital importance. It stated: "Considerable quantities of freight are flown. Almost everything that can fit into an aircraft has been carried. After the introduction of television, over 8,000 sets were flown from Aberdeen to Kirkwall. Other items frequently carried include bicycles, blood-plasma, serums, day-old chicks and spares for vehicles." The working environment came in for comment: "The Station Superintendent not only knows all the crews but also many of the passengers so that the personal touch creates a friendly atmosphere. The islanders regard the air services from a very personal point of view and take a close interest in any problems or developments." Noting that air services were maintained through the worst of weathers, the journal continued: "Many sectors are flown at an altitude of only 1,000 feet. The weather in the north is not always ideal. The two main hazards are sea fog and high winds; on occasion a combination of the two arises with gale force winds and visibility down to yards. Navigation aids are not very advanced."

BEA Handley Page Herald. (Courtesy of the late Captain Ian Montgomery)

Vickers Viscount 1962-1982

This aircraft type was one of the most successful products of Britain's civil aviation industry. In 1953 it had flown the world's first turboprop-powered scheduled airline service. Four Rolls-Royce Darts gave the Viscount V802 a maximum speed of 350 mph and it could carry seventy-four passengers. It also flew occasional charter flights from Kirkwall to Bergen. When the scheduled services to Kirkwall became Viscount-only in October 1966 following withdrawal of the Heralds, one runway at Grimsetter was lengthened to 4,600 feet.

On 31 March 1974 BEA was formally absorbed by British Airways. On 29 May 1974, the fortieth anniversary of the first airmail service of Fresson's Highland Airways was commemorated when the British Airways Vickers Viscount, G-AOHO, flew the regular scheduled service from Inverness to Kirkwall. On 8 May 1982, British Airways withdrew the Viscount from the Scottish domestic network. The last scheduled service was flown by G-AOYM, under callsign *Speedbird 5721*, from Sumburgh to Glasgow via Kirkwall and Inverness.

A busy day on the Kirkwall ramp with three BEA Vickers Viscounts awaiting passengers. (OLPA via Robert Foden)

Vickers Viscount V802, G-AOJE, of British Airways is readied for departure during the early 1980s. (OLPA)

Enter Loganair

In February 1966, Piper Aztec, G-ASER, of Loganair, flown by Captain Ken Foster and Captain Jim Lee (the resident pilot designate for Orkney), visited landing fields in the North Isles preparatory to the start of inter-island services. They were joined by Colonel H W Scarth, County Convenor, and Allan Bullen, the Manager of the Orkney Islands Shipping Company. It was reported that, "At each island landing field, a small hut is being placed for the storage of fire-fighting equipment and the limited shelter of passengers." The original start date was planned for June 1966 and, as the new Britten-Norman Islander aircraft would not be available until the following year, the intention was to use a Dornier Do28A. The proposed single fares to Kirkwall were £2 from Eday and Stronsay, and £2 10s (£2.50) from the other islands. In the event, Piper Aztecs were used until the first Islander was delivered.

William Scarth and Allan Bullen meet Loganair Piper Aztec, G-ASER, c.1967. (OLPA)

On 27 September 1967 Loganair revived internal Orkney air services from Kirkwall to Stronsay, Sanday and North Ronaldsay with the 9-passenger Britten-Norman BN2A Islander, G-AVKC. It was the first airline in the world to operate the Islander for fare-paying scheduled passengers. Initially, the operation was by arrangement with the Orkney Islands Shipping Company (OISC), as this enabled government support given to the shipping company to be made available to the airline. In the first week, seventy passengers were carried. Loganair's first Orkney-based pilot was Captain Jim Lee, who later trained to become a General Practitioner. Loganair also began providing ambulance flights for the North Islands.

Early Loganair inter-island services. Britten-Norman Islander, G-AVRA, during a turnaround on Eday. (OLPA)

Loganair was formed in Edinburgh in 1962 as a small air-taxi operation for the Logan Construction Co Ltd, transporting senior executives and key employees. The fleet expanded along with diversity of operations from aerial photography, to supply dropping on St Kilda, to charter work for Littlewood's Pools. The first scheduled passenger service operated by the airline was from Edinburgh to Dundee in October 1963 using a five-passenger Piper Aztec. This type was also used by Loganair in the very early days of the Orkney inter-island service due to the late delivery of the Islander. On 25 October 1967, Westray and Papa Westray were added to Loganair's inter-island network.

Rousay-bound are Dr John Firth and his brother, Eddie, on Loganair Piper Tri-Pacer, G-ARHV, during the early 1960s.

Seven thousand passengers were carried in the first year of renewed inter-island services. Mail was also carried occasionally. In 1968, the company was bought by the National Commercial Bank of Scotland, which, after a merger, became the Royal Bank of Scotland.

Islands and Islanders

One of Loganair's pilots was Captain Arthur Kerr. He recalled some of his early experiences: "Not long after I became a line pilot, the scheduled run had to be made in rather poor weather. Not knowing all the local landmarks, I soon got lost. So I threw the chart to the passengers and said, 'you've been here more often than me, so show me where we are and I'll carry on.'" He gained the necessary knowledge quickly. "Tide demarcation marks, red barn doors, lines of telegraph poles, a broken down tractor in a field, or a particular coastal rock formation. Navigation quickly became a case of reading the landmarks." There were some unique hazards. "The landing strips were often covered in mud and sharn (from cows). The sharn also got into the air intakes for the aircraft heating systems where it began to cook and fill the aircraft with a pretty foul stench at times." Sometimes night ambulance flights had a larger audience than expected. "When I turned for take-off in the glare of the tractor lights illuminating the airstrip, the aircraft's lights picked up hundreds and hundreds of eyes staring at me – Sanday's rabbit population."

This sequence of shots of a Loganair Islander illustrate the sometimes challenging conditions encountered on island airstrips.
(Courtesy of Loganair, Kirkwall)

During the 1970 General Election, ballot boxes were once more transferred by air from the islands to Kirkwall for the votes to be counted. Later the same year, Loganair was authorised by the Post Office to carry inter-island 1st and 2nd class post, commencing on 23 November to North Ronaldsay, Sanday, Stronsay and Westray, and the next day to Papa Westray in Islander, G-AVKC.

London Airport, on Eday, so called because of its location near the Bay of London, opened on 3 May 1971 permitting the extension of passenger and mail services to the island.

In 1972, the fares to Eday and Stronsay remained at £2, Sanday, North Ronaldsay, Westray, and Papa Westray £2 10s (£2.50), and between the islands £1.

An early Loganair inter-island timetable. This indicates the important role played by the Orkney Isles Shipping Company.

O.I.S.C.

A Loganair Islander makes its approach to Stronsay's airstrip. (OLPA)

NORTH ISLES AIR SERVICE
TIMETABLE

loganair ltd

On 24 November 1972, Loganair made its first landing on Hoy. In 1973, Loganair was awarded an Air Ambulance contract by the Scottish Home and Health Department following BEA's disposal of its DH114 Herons. Heavily involved in the development of local scheduled services and air ambulance provision during the 1970s was the Senior Pilot in Orkney, Captain Andy Alsop. He was keen to commemorate special events, which he did with philatelic First Day Covers, flown in the aircraft and signed by the captain. He also recalls that, for a short time after the Heron retired, BEA used the Short Skyliner for Air Ambulance flights. Loganair's first inflight birth occurred on 2 August 1973 at 2,000 feet above Kirkwall, on the way to Aberdeen from Stronsay. The mother was Mrs Freida Devin, and baby Kathy was given the additional name 'Leynair' in honour of Captain Jamie Bay*ley* and Loga*nair*. On 16 October 1973, the first scheduled service to Hoy (Longhope) was flown in Islander, G-AXVR. On 16 September 1975, the 100,000th inter-island passenger, Miss Harriet Kirkness, was presented with a silver bracelet by Christine Allan, who still works with Loganair as Senior Customer Services Officer at Kirkwall Airport.

Above: BEA's two Short Skyliner aircraft nearing completion in Belfast. (Short Brothers Ltd / Bombardier Aerospace Belfast)

Island People

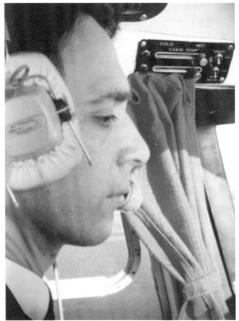

Loganair's Andy Alsop at the yoke. (Courtesy of Loganair, Kirkwall)

Opposite top. *Captain Keith Alderson and Loganair's de Havilland Canada DHC-6 at Kirkwall. (Courtesy of Loganair, Glasgow)*

Opposite bottom. *Tom Miller at ease at Papa Westray's terminal where he was the station manager. (Courtesy of Loganair, Glasgow)*

'*Ready, Andy? Take 1!*' *Inter-island services have consistently attracted the interest of journalists and broadcasters. (Courtesy of Loganair, Glasgow)*

British Airways' Budgie
Hawker Siddeley 748 1975-1992

Like the Vickers Viscount and the Handley Page Herald, this Avro design was also powered by Rolls-Royce Dart turboprop engines and could carry a full load of forty-four passengers on the most demanding sectors of British Airways' Scottish network. It first flew in 1960, the manufacturer's original aim being to provide a replacement for the Douglas DC-3, though in the event, its main sales rival was the Fokker F27 Friendship. It was a commercially successful design, with more than 370 being sold worldwide. British Airways bought two Series 2A HS748s for its Highland Division in 1975 and three Series 2Bs in 1984-85. It also leased twelve others at different times during the years 1982 to 1992.

The first HS748 in British Airways service was G-BCOE, *Glen Livet / Gleann Liomhaid.* Delivered on 10 July 1975, it went into service on 4 August 1975 on the Glasgow–Aberdeen–Kirkwall–Sumburgh route. The HS748 was a rugged and economic aircraft that was also employed on crew change operations for the Occidental Oil Terminal at Flotta. A seasonal scheduled service from Kirkwall to Bergen commenced on 6 June 1987. There were many local events to commemorate the 850th anniversary of St Magnus Cathedral and these included the temporary naming of British Airways HS748 aircraft, G-BGJV as *St Magnus of Orkney.* It was christened with Orkney-distilled *Highland Park* whisky prior to the inaugural Bergen flight.

The HS748 also visited Orkney carrying members of the Royal Family as an aircraft of The Queen's Flight. In its military role it was known as the Andover, and was flown by RAF Transport Command as a tactical freighter and VIP transport.

British Airways Hawker Siddeley, G-BCOF, Glen Fiddich / Gleann Fithich. *(British Airways)*

Opposite top: A New Year snow fall, January 1982. (Robert Foden)

Opposite bottom: A Loganair Islander is besieged by HS748s of British Airways and the Queen's Flight. (Michael Firth)

Loganair, oil, and engineering

On 1 May 1976, the first Loganair scheduled service from Inverness to Wick and Kirkwall was flown by Islander G-AXSS. This route had been taken over from British Airways. The first landing on Flotta was made by Islander, G-AWNR, on 28 May 1976.

Also in 1976, all Islander maintenance for Loganair became centred at Kirkwall. It is probable that the present Base Engineer for Loganair at Kirkwall knows as much about maintaining Islanders as anyone else in the world, as Bryan Sutherland has been there since Loganair's arrival in 1967. A further development came in 1977 when Loganair assumed sole responsibility for inter-island air services, marking an end to the involvement of the Orkney Islands Shipping Company. On 1 March 1977 the first scheduled service to Flotta via Hoy was flown by Islander, G-AXVR.

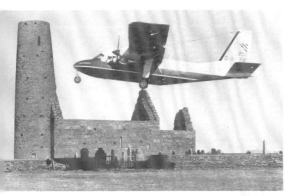

Loganair Islander, G-AYXK, Captain Eric A Starling, *makes a descent past St Magnus Church on Egilsay. (OLPA)*

Approach to the rocky shore-line of North Ronaldsay. (OLPA)

Loganair Managing Director Captain Duncan McIntosh (far left), Conservative Party leader Margaret Thatcher, and Captain Andy Alsop mark the 10th anniversary of inter-island services. (OLPA via Robert Foden)

The Flotta Oil Terminal was opened by the Energy Minister, Tony Benn MP, on 11 January 1977. In the same year, the 10th anniversary of Loganair's inter-island services was celebrated with 135,000 passengers having been carried in that time. Visiting Kirkwall that day was Mrs Margaret Thatcher, then leader of the Conservative Party in opposition, who joined in, cut the birthday cake and handed it around the assembled guests. These included Desmond Norman and his wife. Desmond Norman, along with John Britten, designed and manufactured the Britten-Norman Islander. Loganair was the first operator of the Islander and more than 1,250 have been built, many of them flying in the most difficult operating environments. On 23 February 1979, the first landing on Egilsay was made by Islander, G-AYXK. By 1981 Loganair scheduled services to Hoy had come to an end because of the boggy conditions at the airstrip, while those to Flotta were discontinued as a direct result of free ferry services being provided by the oil company.

Islander G-AWNR passing the Old Man of Hoy. (OLPA via Robert Foden)

Energy Minister Tony Benn (far left) at Kirkwall for the opening of the Flotta Oil Terminal. (Courtesy of Janette Ridgway)

The Oil Boom

The opening of the terminal on Flotta was not the only oil-related stimulus to air transport in Orkney. Oil workers flew to Kirkwall by Dan-Air charter and were then taken to Unst (the most northerly of the Shetland Islands) by Loganair Britten-Norman Trislanders and de Havilland Canada DHC-6 Twin Otters. The Trislander was a development of the Islander with an increased passenger capacity of sixteen and a third engine mounted on the tail fin. The Twin Otter, which was manufactured by de Havilland Canada, is a rugged twin-engine turboprop with excellent short take-off and landing capabilities.

Loganair's Britten-Norman Trislander G-BDKR. (David Dyer)

Kirkwall ramp in the late 1970s – Loganair Twin Otters and Islanders and a British Airways Viscount. (OLPA via Robert Foden)

A Loganair Twin Otter. This all-red example was leased from British Antarctic Survey. (OLPA)

On 25 October 1979, a mishap occurred when, in a landing accident, the Guernsey Airways/Alidair Viscount, G-BFYZ, operating an oil industry charter service, ran off the runway at Kirkwall, fortunately without serious injury to the forty-seven passengers and four crew. In the early 1980s, weather diversions from Sumburgh in Shetland were a common occurrence. With the major upsurge in traffic due to the oil boom, Kirkwall could become quite crowded. The busiest day saw over 1,000 passengers at the airport.

A dramatic halt for Guernsey Airlines' Viscount, G-BFYZ.
(Courtesy of Robert Milne)

The intensity of oil-related activity is conveyed by this line-up of support aircraft at Kirkwall. (Michael Firth)

Loganair in the 1980s

The decade began with an unfortunate incident when, in February 1980, Islander, G-BFCX, had to be airlifted from Rousay by helicopter, Sikorsky S-61, G-BDIJ, after landing in wet and windy conditions and coming to rest in a ditch.

Following a bumpy landing on Rousay, Islander G-BFCX was given a lift to Kirkwall for repairs. (OLPA)

*Loganair Embraer
Bandeirante, G-BHHA.
(David Dyer)*

*Loganair Shorts 330,
G-BGNA.
(David Dyer Collection)*

*Shorts 360, G-LEGS. Dual
Loganair and Manx
Airlines markings, and a
registration that reinforces
a crisis of identity.
(Iain Hutchison)*

Later that year Loganair started an Edinburgh to Kirkwall service using a
Shorts 330 and this incorporated a stop at Wick from 1981. The Shorts SD3-30
was designed and constructed by Short Brothers of Belfast. It was a sturdy,
practical, but rather boxy aeroplane, with twin tail fins. It could carry thirty-
three passengers. Occasional services were also flown by the smaller
Brazilian-built Embraer EMB110 Bandeirante, which had a passenger capacity
of eighteen. In December 1983, Loganair became part of the Airlines of Britain
Group, joining forces with British Midland and Manx Airlines. It was acquired
by British Midland (75%) and Loganair's Managing Director, Scott Grier
(25%), subsequently becoming a wholly owned subsidiary of Airlines of
Britain Holdings plc in 1987.

In 1984, Loganair introduced the Shorts 360 to the Kirkwall-Wick-Edinburgh service. The Shorts 360 was developed from the Shorts 330, it had a single tail fin and an increased passenger capacity of thirty-six. Along with its predecessor, it made a very important contribution to the development of regional air services. To begin with, services were shared with nineteen-seat Twin Otters. The Shorts 360 took over fully in 1989, with the Twin Otter being used again in 1991. By 1993, Loganair was flying the Kirkwall-Edinburgh route with the British Aerospace ATP.

Loganair's Twin Otter upon arrival from Edinburgh, February 1982.
(Robert Foden)

Loganair ATP, G-OLCC, seen at Glasgow in 1990. (Iain Hutchison)

In 1985, air ambulance strips were established on Egilsay, Wyre and Shapinsay, but ambulance services to these islands, and Hoy, have now been discontinued. The earliest record that Andy Alsop could find in his log book of a flight to Shapinsay was in September 1976. Only Hoy had a proper airstrip. Flotta still has a hard runway, but it is very seldom used.

A wet and windy descent conveys the challenges faced by Islander pilots during this approach to the airstrip on Fair Isle. (Author)

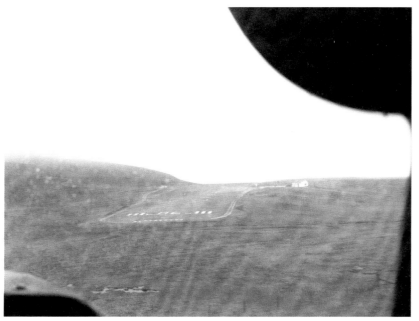

In 1986, a Kirkwall-Fair Isle service with the ubiquitous Islander was started. The island, which is situated between Orkney and Shetland, is the home to thousands upon thousands of seabirds and is owned by the National Trust for Scotland. It is justifiably world-renowned by ornithologists. The first ever landing by an aeroplane on the island was made on 13 May 1937 by Ted Fresson, in his Monospar, G-ACEW, while the island's children were given a special Christmas treat in 1937 when John Hankins landed dressed as Santa Claus to distribute presents.

Loganair carried a very unusual cargo on a series of scheduled flights during 1986 when hedgehogs, which had become a pest to nesting birds on the islands of North Ronaldsay and Papa Westray, were flown to Edinburgh via Kirkwall as part of a dispersal programme.

Air Orkney

In 1981, the charter company Air Orkney was established by local businessmen. The well-known former Loganair pilot, Captain Andy Alsop, was the Chief Pilot. He took up another flying job in the Falkland Islands in 1983 and was succeeded by Ed Bewley. During its first year of operation, Air Orkney completed 273 charter contracts involving 791 landings and the carriage of 2,828 passengers, visiting nearly fifty airfields throughout Scotland and the islands. Britten-Norman Islander, G-AXXG, came to grief on top of Carn Sleamhuim in the Cairngorms, a few miles west of Aviemore, on 24 March 1983 when it ran out of fuel and had to make a forced landing. It was being flown by a ferry pilot returning the aircraft after its annual maintenance checks at Perth. G-AXXG was replaced by another Islander, G-BESO, which was acquired from Jersey European Airways in June 1983. The company folded after only a few years in business and G-BESO was leased to Loganair in June 1984 prior to being sold.

Air Orkney Islander, G-AXXG. (Courtesy of B-N Historians)

G-AXXG was succeeded by G-BESO. (Courtesy of B-N Historians)

Right: An evocative scene after G-AXXG has come to rest in the Cairngorm Mountains. (OLPA)

Farewell to the Viscount

On 27 and 28 March 1982, British Airways operated special flights from Glasgow to Kirkwall with Vickers Viscounts G-AOYL, G-AOYM, G-AOYO, and G-APIM, to mark the airline's withdrawal of the type twenty-five years after it had first visited Kirkwall and following twenty years of scheduled services. Three hundred passengers, many of whom were British Airways air crew and ground crew, past and present, took part in the occasion, which included a celebratory dinner and dance in Kirkwall. The instigator and chief organiser of this very popular and fondly remembered event was Jack Ridgway, who was to serve for nearly twenty years as BEA and British Airways Station Manager at the airport. Hundreds of spectators watched as the four aircraft departed at lunchtime on Sunday 28 March, each making a low flypast of the airport and the town.

£1.50 for a dance! (Courtesy of Janette Ridgway)

Final Viscount line-up at Kirkwall, 28 March 1982.
(Photo: H Peace, courtesy of Janette Ridgway)

British Airways

Viscount Farewell Dance
with the BRAELANDERS

in the
ALBERT BALLROOM
on Saturday 27th March 1982

9.30 p.m.—1.30 a.m.

Ticket £1.50

A lament for the Viscounts? (Photo: H Peace, courtesy of Janette Ridgway)

Opposite top: A Viscount over Kirkwall. (OLPA)
Opposite bottom: Final departure, 28 March 1982. (Robert Foden)

The Advanced Turboprop

The British Aerospace Advanced Turboprop (ATP) took over from the Hawker Siddeley HS748 in British Airways service in 1988. It resembles a stretched version of its predecessor, with a longer fuselage, a more pointed nose, revised wingtips, and a redesigned swept fin and rudder. It is equipped with a pair of fuel-efficient Pratt & Whitney Canada PW126A turboprops driving quiet six-bladed propellers, has a faster cruising speed, and an advanced flightdeck with digital avionics and flight information presented on electronic multifunction display screens - the 'glass cockpit'. It has a passenger capacity of sixty-four and, from a passenger viewpoint, the ATP is a comfortable aeroplane in which to fly with low noise levels. It made its first flight on 6 August 1986 and entered airline service less than two years later with British Midland. Disappointingly for the manufacturers, it did not sell in great numbers, with only sixty-four being produced, but after some initial teething problems it gave useful service on routes to Kirkwall until 1996, flown successively by British Airways, Loganair and British Regional Airlines. In recent years, several ATPs have been converted to freighter configuration and have performed well in this role.

British Airways ATP, G-BTPK, at Kirkwall embarking guests attending the sixtieth anniversary of the Orkney air mail. About to climb the steps is Captain Eric Starling who joined Aberdeen Airways as chief pilot in 1934. (Iain Hutchison)

Loganair ATP, G-LOGA, and Shorts 360, G-WACK, cross paths at Belfast City Airport. (Short Brothers Ltd / Bombardier Aerospace Belfast)

Loganair in the early 1990s

During nearly forty years of service to Orkney, Loganair has used a wide range of aircraft types which have included the Piper Aztec, Beech 18, Britten-Norman Islander, Short Skyvan, de Havilland Canada DHC-6 Twin Otter, Shorts 330, Embraer Bandeirante, Britten-Norman Trislander, Shorts 360, British Aerospace Jetstream 31, British Aerospace Jetstream 41, British Aerospace ATP and Saab 340.

  In October 1991, a Glasgow to Kirkwall service with British Aerospace Jetstream 31s started. The Jetstream 31 is a sleek twin-engine turboprop which can carry nineteen passengers. By 1993, Loganair's services from Orkney were operated by BAe ATP to Edinburgh and Sumburgh, BAe Jetstream 31 to Inverness and Glasgow and Britten-Norman Islander to Wick and Fair Isle. In that year, a seasonal summer Loganair schedule from Kirkwall to Bergen was started and used the Jetstream 41, a 29-passenger development of the Jetstream 31.

The BAe Jetstream 31 enabled Loganair to operate non-stop flights between Glasgow, where G-LOGU is seen in 1991, and Kirkwall. (Iain Hutchison)

Jetstream 41, G-LOGL, at Bergen in 1993 while operating the scheduled service from Kirkwall. (Robert Foden)

63

Loganair Shorts 360, G-BLGB, at Kirkwall in British Airways' 'Landor' livery.

The Loganair inter-island check-in desk at Kirkwall also succumbed to a British Airways identity.

Loganair Shorts 360 and Islander at Kirkwall following implementation of the 1994 British Airways franchise arrangement.

Pre-Millennium Developments

Reorganisation within the Airlines of Britain Group resulted in Loganair's BAe ATPs and BAe Jetstream 41s passing to Manx Airlines (Europe). So once more the Shorts 360 became the mainstay of services to Orkney. On 11 July 1994, Loganair became a British Airways franchise operator. During 1995-96, Manx Airlines took over the management of the Loganair operation, although the identity of Loganair was retained for corporate purposes. Later that year Manx Airlines' UK mainland services became British Regional Airlines (BRAL) and many of Loganair's operations were incorporated. At this time, British Airways passed its remaining Scottish internal routes to BRAL for operation under a franchise agreement under the name British Airways Express.

In February 1997, Loganair re-emerged as an independent company following a management buy-out led by Managing Director, Scott Grier, which included all Britten-Norman Islander and DHC Twin Otter operations within the Highlands and Islands, as well as the specialist services for the Scottish Air Ambulance. By December 1997, British Regional Airlines was flying from Kirkwall to Aberdeen, Edinburgh, Glasgow, Sumburgh, Inverness and Wick with ATPs and Shorts 360s. Loganair acquired the Saab 340B in 1999 and used it to replace the Shorts 360 on the Glasgow-Inverness-Kirkwall service. The thirty-four seat Swedish-built Saab first flew in 1983 and sold well in the difficult US market.

Below:
A Shorts 360 shares the
summer sunshine with the
landscape at Grimsetter.

Above: A Loganair Saab
340 displays a further
change of identity under
British Airways. Also on the
ramp are a Shorts 360,
Britten-Norman Islander,
and BAe ATP.
(All photos: Michael Firth)

Services to the islands in the 21st century

In recent times, the outer islands have been provided with gravel runways to a standard length of 465 metres, the maximum requirement for the greatest all-up weight of the aircraft. Previously, the existing grass strips were prone to becoming muddy. Indeed, as they also doubled up as cow pastures, mud was not the only substance that had to be washed off the Islander twice or three times daily. Sometimes turning into the wind for take-off could be more accurately described as churning into the mud.

In the course of a typical year some 18,000 passengers use the island airfields. While tourists visit Eday, Stronsay, Sanday, Westray, Papa Westray and North Ronaldsay for their beauty, tranquillity and abundant flora and fauna, the islanders are frequent flyers. Bank officials, teachers, vets, repair men, and political representatives are some of the most regular visitors. Islanders find the air service convenient for visiting Kirkwall for secondary schooling, appointments and shopping. Necessities such as mail, newspapers, and spare parts for generators, milking machines or tractors, are important cargo items. The age profile of those carried has ranged from over 100 years old to those born in flight.

Islander G-BJOP parked on a snowy apron at Papa Westray. (Ian Potten)

Loganair Islander G-BLNW and the monument to Ted Fresson. (Author)

Cockpit view of another wintery arrival, this time on North Ronaldsay. (Ian Potten)

The distance from Westray to Papa Westray is 1.3 miles (2.09 km), or from terminal to terminal 1.75 miles (2.81 km), much less than the length of London Heathrow's runways which are two and a half miles long (4.02 km). The windsock at the destination airfield is clearly visible from the departing aircraft before take-off. The timetabled duration is two minutes, but is often much less with a favourable wind, making it the shortest scheduled airline flight in the world. A time of 69 seconds recorded by Captain Andy Alsop to mark the acknowledgement of the service by the *Guinness Book of Records* was later reduced by him to 58 seconds.

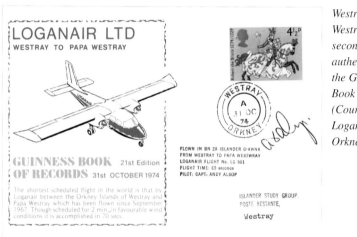

Westray to Papa Westray in 69 seconds, authenticated by the Guinness Book of Records. (Courtesy of Loganair, Orkney)

In 2001, a national Sunday newspaper ran a feature article headed 'Diary of a day with the Flying Bankers'. It described in some detail a day in the lives of Anne Rendall, the Cashier at the Royal Bank of Scotland in Kirkwall, and its Business Manager, Kenny Flett. Anne's normal working routine was detailed as flying to Westray twice a week, once to Stronsay, with another day on Sanday, while North Ronaldsay was visited twice a month and Papa Westray once. On the islands, she opens up the branch office and conducts all normal banking business for the islanders. Anne estimated that she had made about 3,500 flights between the islands over the previous six years. What the article failed to highlight was the long term commitment to this unique service made by the Bank and Loganair since 1969. Perhaps the best known banker was Miss Maisie Muir, who hailed from Sanday, and who averaged 528 flights a year between 1969 and 1987. By the time of her final trip, on 5 May 1987, Miss Muir had logged 8,400 inter-island flights.

Loganair as Orkney's mainline airline

In September 2001, British Regional Airlines withdrew from Kirkwall leaving Loganair, operating Saab 340s, to provide all scheduled services from Orkney as a British Airways franchise holder. Loganair is therefore now a crucial link for the islands.

Loganair's Saab 340 on the tarmac at Kirkwall. (Author)

A Saab 340 cabin attendant awaits the imminent embarkation of passengers at Wick. (Author)

The ground operation at Kirkwall continues to be controlled by British Airways staff under the management of Robert Milne who has been with the company at Kirkwall for thirty-five years. Alongside Robert and his team in the new terminal, completed in 2001, is the Loganair operation, which has maintained the Orkney inter-island services since 1967 and whose Islanders reverted to Loganair livery in 2004 after flying in British Airways colours from 1994.

Christine Allan, Loganair Senior Customer Services Officer, Kirkwall. (Neil Thain)

Neil Thain, Facilities Manager, Kirkwall Airport. (Lorraine Campbell / Neil Thain)

Robert Milne,
British Airways
Airport
Manager,
Kirkwall.
(Neil Thain)

David
Blackman,
Kirkwall Airport
Manager.
(Neil Thain)

Another very long-serving employee at Kirkwall is Loganair's Senior Customer Services Officer, Christine Allan, who has completed more than thirty years service. Six times every weekday and four times on Saturdays, an Islander takes off from Kirkwall to the outer islands. Most flights call at two islands before returning to Kirkwall. The most distant, North Ronaldsay, is 33 miles (53 km) away, while the closest, Stronsay, is 16 miles (25.7 km) distant. Sector times are short, with no flight being more than 15 minutes, the quickest from Westray to Papa Westray being scheduled at two minutes.

Loganair offers a modern, more comfortable version of the inter-island service pioneered by Ted Fresson between 1934 and 1939. This would not have been possible without the remarkable Britten-Norman Islander, which Loganair has used on these routes since 1967. It remains the perfect aircraft for the job, well-loved and trusted by pilots, passengers and engineers alike. It is rugged and durable, easy to maintain with simple systems. It has an excellent single-engine performance in the unlikely event that this should be required. The Textron Lycoming 195 kw 0-540 piston engines start like a dream and do not object to the frequent stops and re-starts required. The short field performance of the Islander is well-known and appreciated worldwide. Less remarked upon, but equally useful, is its broad centre of gravity envelope, which greatly facilitates swift loading. The wide doors are also a plus factor, as some of the passengers may be elderly or infirm and some of the items transported can be bulky or awkwardly shaped. The fixed under-carriage withstands the short hops and multiple landings with ease and, with less moving parts than in retractable undercarriages, mal-functions are rare. It is a worthy successor to the renowned DH89.

A Loganair Islander in the colours of the Scottish Ambulance Service on a wintery North Ronaldsay. (Ian Potten)

Islander G-BLDV catches the sun outside the Kirkwall maintenance hangar. (Author)

Loganair always has two aircraft ready for action, one operating the scheduled services, while the other is on standby for air ambulance duties. A good proportion of these mercy flights are routine in nature, but some are urgent night missions in marginal weather, with the patient's life being in the hands of the pilot and the doctor or paramedic on board. Loganair has been flying on

behalf of the Scottish Air Ambulance Service since 1967, taking over the complete contract from BEA in 1973, carrying on the great tradition of Captains David Barclay, Henry Vallance and Eric Starling to name but a few. No praise can be too high for the company's fine record of airmanship and dedication to the task.

Above: Loganair's Islanders have recovered their own identity following withdrawal of single-pilot operated aircraft from the British Airways franchise arrangement. (Author)

Kirkwall movements

Saab 340 schedules are flown to Edinburgh, Glasgow, Sumburgh, Inverness, Aberdeen and Wick throughout the year, with seasonal variations. Royal Mail is flown to Kirkwall six days a week in a Let L-410 of the Danish airline Benair on the routes Kinloss-Kirkwall–Inverness, and Aberdeen-Sumburgh-Kirkwall-Aberdeen.

A Let 410 of Benair on a mail flight at Kirkwall, April 2004.
(Robert Foden)

Highland Airways of Inverness (named in honour of Ted Fresson's company and with its Head Office in Kerrogair House, once occupied by Fresson himself) carries the newspapers every day in Rheims Cessna F406 Caravan II, G-LEAF, or BAe Jetstreams, G-BTXG, G-JURA and G-UIST. Highland Airways also uses the Jetstreams for charter flights, and undertakes Fishery Protection and reconnaissance duties over Scotland's territorial waters with Cessna F406s G-SFPA and G-SFPB. Another Caravan II, G-TWIG, was a regular visitor with newspapers from 1998 until 2004 when it crashed during a flight from Stornoway to Inverness.

The main runway 09/27 at Kirkwall has a length of 4,698 feet (1,432 metres), VOR/DME and, since June 2004, an Instrument Landing System (ILS). The introduction of ILS has dramatically reduced the number of cancelled or delayed flights due to bad weather. The other runways are 06/24, which is 3,881 feet (1,183 metres) long but has a weight limitation of 12,568 lbs (5,700 kg) MTWA, and 15/33 which is 2,230 feet (680 metres) in length.

Cessna Caravan, G-TWIG, in preparation for a newspaper run at Inverness. (Highland Airways)

BAe Jetstream 31, G-JURA, of Highland Airways. (Highland Airways)

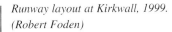

Runway layout at Kirkwall, 1999. (Robert Foden)

A BAe146 of the Royal Flight provides the rare visit of a 'large' jet to Kirkwall. (Neil Thain)

Opposite:
1 Eurocopter EC135, G-SASB, operated by Bond Helicopters for the Scottish Ambulance Service. (Neil Thain)
2 MBB Bo105 of North Scottish Helicopters operating on behalf of the Northern Lighthouse Board to supply lighthouses, 1982. All Scottish lighthouses are now fully automatic. (Robert Foden)
3 Sikorsky S76, G-BOND, of Northern Scottish, a weather diversion from Sumburgh in 1983. (Robert Foden)
4 Sikorsky S61s of Bristow Helicopters G-BDOC and G-BDII operating for HM Coastguard and visiting Kirkwall for a photo shoot in 1987. (Robert Foden)
5 Aerospatiale Super Puma G-PUMN of CHC Helicopters at Kirkwall, September 2001. (Iain Hutchison)
6 British Airways provided extra offshore lifting power with the Boeing Vertol Chinook, another 1983 weather diversion from Sumburgh . (Robert Foden)

1

2

3

4

5

6

77

Flying around the Islands

The islands to the north of Kirkwall are mostly low lying and green, with neat fields stretching to the shoreline. Dry stone walls enclose sheep and cow pastures, except on North Ronaldsay - where the encircling stone dyke keeps the unique island breed of sheep on the outside, on a diet of seaweed, which renders its flesh ready-salted. Farms, hamlets and churches lie serenely under the big skies, seals bask on the rocks below, while seabirds nest in profusion.

For a tour of the north isles, in 2001 I joined the Duty Pilot, Ian Potten, one of four based at Kirkwall, the others at that time being Senior Pilot, Stuart Linklater, and Captains Dave Kirkland and Malcolm Hempsell. Ian had more than 7,000 hours in his logbook on DC-3s with Air Atlantique, flying ATPs out of Belfast City for Loganair, and three and a half years on Islanders in Shetland before transferring to Orkney. Obviously happy with his job, he said: "There are few other airline posts in the world where you can live in the countryside and

still be within walking distance of work. In the air I have a 100-mile view out over the islands to Fair Isle and Foula on the horizon. The sea and the sky are ever-changing shades of blue and grey, while the land is picked out in pastel shades of purple, brown and green." All flying is VFR, hands on, without the autopilot being engaged. Generally, the maximum ceiling is 1,000 feet (304 metres), with much flying being at 500 feet (152 metres) and speeds around 120 kts (222 kph). The limiting factors for scheduled flights are maintenance of a height not below 400 feet (122 metres), with an inflight visibility of no less than 1.8 miles (3.04 km) and a crosswind no more than 20 kts (37 kph). The most important factor is the taxi limit of 50 kts (92 kph), as in winds as high as that, landings into wind are made at a groundspeed of below 20 kts (37 kph).

Service as usual despite an inclement day on Fair Isle. (Author)

Opposite: Loganair's Captain Ian Potten about to set off from Kirkwall on a regular inter-island run. (Author)

Approach to a typical island airstrip. This one is on Stronsay. (Author)

The chief problems are winds in winter and fog in summer. The lore of wind and tide is of great use to today's island pilot. Just like the old-time flying boat captains, they study wave patterns on approach to assist in judging wind strength and direction for landing. The pilot is responsible for all decisions as he makes his way from island to island. Kirkwall Air Traffic Control (ATC) on 118.3 MHz controls activity at the main airport, and a weather advisory service is also available. The outer islands are not, however, in controlled airspace. On approach, and prior to departure, the pilot radios his intentions, but the decision-making is his alone. Inbound to Kirkwall, he advises ATC that he is ten miles out and crossing the coast of Shapinsay. At that stage, the clearly visible landmarks of the two hangars at Kirkwall come into view, and the pilot also reports to the office on his fuel status and enquires about the passenger figures for the next three sectors. He can then decide on the quantity of fuel he wishes to uplift. A lot of responsibility is vested in the pilot and the job requires skill, maturity and experience.

Kirkwall has permanent lighting, but portable aids only are available for the other airstrips, except for North Ronaldsay, which has permanent lights for air ambulance flights only. The only other indicators on the islands are red marks painted on the dry stone walls at each end of the runway. Therefore all scheduled flights to the outer islands must be completed before dusk.

The Orkney inter-island experience is a highly memorable one, and not just for the flying, but also for the unique personal touch from the pre-flight briefing given by the captain turning around in his seat to address the passengers, to the personal handling of 95% of bookings by either Christine Allan, or her assistant, Petrina Thomson, who may also be seen collecting the boarding cards or wheeling the baggage trolley.

A vintage car at London Airport, Eday, gives a timeless air to this study of G-BLNW on a regular schedule. (Author)

Opposite: North Ronaldsay. (Author)

Loganair issues these colourful souvenir tickets to island hoppers.

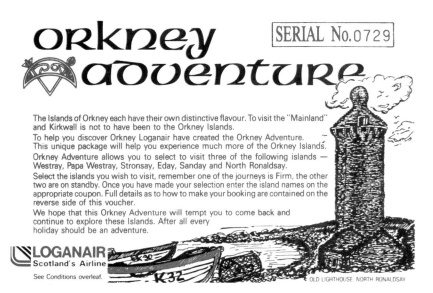

orkney
adventure

SERIAL No.0729

The Islands of Orkney each have their own distinctive flavour. To visit the "Mainland" and Kirkwall is not to have been to the Orkney Islands.

To help you discover Orkney Loganair have created the Orkney Adventure. This unique package will help you experience much more of the Orkney Islands.

Orkney Adventure allows you to select to visit three of the following islands — Westray, Papa Westray, Stronsay, Eday, Sanday and North Ronaldsay.

Select the islands you wish to visit, remember one of the journeys is Firm, the other two are on standby. Once you have made your selection enter the island names on the appropriate coupon. Full details as to how to make your booking are contained on the reverse side of this voucher.

We hope that this Orkney Adventure will tempt you to come back and continue to explore these Islands. After all every holiday should be an adventure.

LOGANAIR
Scotland's Airline

See Conditions overleaf.

OLD LIGHTHOUSE NORTH RONALDSAY

The World's Shortest Flight

One of the attractions to flying round the islands is the opportunity to fly on the world's shortest scheduled airline flight. This is the sector between Westray and Papa Westray where departing passengers frequently watch their plane coming into land, not at the airport where they will emplane but at the previous airfield across the strait that divides the two islands. The short hop is nothing unusual for islanders who use their air service like a local bus, but visitors might mark their journey on this unusual flight by requesting a commemorative certificate which will be signed by their pilot.

The air terminal on Westray. (Author)

Opposite, top: Approach to Westray airfield with Papa Westray beyond. (Iain Hutchison)

Opposite, bottom: Papa Westray airfield. (Iain Hutchison)

A 'shortest flight' commemorative certificate. (Iain Hutchison)

Loganair's Islander G-BJOP awaits passengers, and mail, at Papa Westray. (Iain Hutchison)

Kirkwall Termination

Kirkwall's air travellers have used various departure points over the years, beginning with Ted Fresson's grass landing site at Wideford Farm. During World War Two, the Royal Naval Air Station at Hatston was made available to passenger flights.

In April 1948, RAF Grimsetter passed to the civilian authorities and replaced Hatston as the civil airport for Orkney. Hatston was deemed too small for BEA's DC-3s which the company intended to introduce. A plan to widen Hatston's runways to facilitate the return of BEA was not followed through. From 1953 to 1957, the airfield at Hatston was used by the Orkney Flying Club. It was then finally closed and turned into an industrial estate.

Informal boarding procedures for Dakota passengers chatting to a staff member in front of the former RAF watch room during the 1950s. (OLPA via Robert Foden)

In 1964 the terminal showed little signs of change from World War Two when Grimsetter was an RAF station. (OLPA)

Firefighting cover at Kirkwall is demonstrated in this vintage shot. (Courtesy of Janette Ridgway)

For many years the terminal buildings at Grimsetter consisted of four nissen huts and the terminal that served until 1969 was converted from the wartime administration block. These buildings may have been utilitarian, but the BEA bus from Kirkwall to the airport was, however, a very popular innovation.

A new passenger terminal was opened at Kirkwall Airport by Jo Grimond MP on 8 April 1969. This was not before time and had been proposed more than once during the previous twenty years. On 18 June 1976, a memorial to Captain E E Fresson was unveiled by his widow, Gwen Fresson, at Kirkwall Airport. She also visited Eday. Ted Fresson died in 1963, while his rival, Eric Gandar Dower, passed away in 1987.

Jo Grimmond marks the official opening of the new terminal in 1969. (courtesy of Janette Ridgway);

The new terminal was to serve Grimsetter for more than three decades. (OLPA via Robert Foden);

The evolution from adapted wartime aerodrome to modern civil airport. (OLPA via Robert Foden)

Airport People

BEA staff c.1969: Harry (Taffy) Fisher, Don Macleod, Jack Watson, John Wood, Jimmy Steen and Brian Kemp. (OLPA via Robert Foden)

'In the tower' in the early 1980s are Geoff Greavey and Janet Firminger. (OLPA via Robert Foden)

Gwen Fresson, widow of the air pioneer, Ted Fresson, visited Eday on 18 June 1976. Andy Alsop looks on as Gwen receives a floral gift. (OLPA via Robert Foden)

Fifty years of Orkney air services. Jo Grimmond addresses the crowd from the Fresson memorial. Jack Ridgway, British Airways Station Manager, is to Jo's right. (OLPA)

On 23 April 1998, a new control tower at Kirkwall was opened. This was followed by the completion of a new passenger terminal on 25 November 2001, officially opened in March 2002. The passenger yearly total in 2004 was 115,000 with some 12,000 aircraft movements.

The dawn of the twenty-first century brought a new terminal with a link to Orkney's Nordic past. The Runic script of the Vikings above the door reads Grimsetter. *(Neil Thain)*

The Fresson memorial, long an airside landmark for passengers boarding their aircraft, is now located in front of the new terminal. (Author)

The interior of the new terminal is a far cry from the days of Grimsetter's nissen hut accommodation. (Neil Thain)

EGPA KOI SCOTLAND

No1 AIDU (RAF) European Aeronautical Group Aerad EGPAD1   Changes Editorial

| Elev 58 | Var 5°W | ARP | N58 57 47 W002 54 30 (WGS 84) | 14 APR 05 | D1 |

| KIRKWALL TOWER 118·3 | ATIS 108·6 |

W002 54   W002 53·

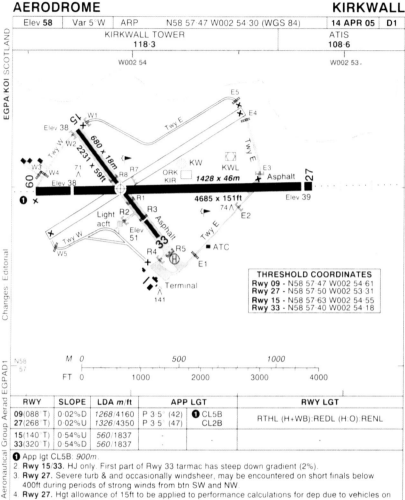

THRESHOLD COORDINATES
Rwy 09 - N58 57 47 W002 54 61
Rwy 27 - N58 57 50 W002 53 31
Rwy 15 - N58 57 63 W002 54 55
Rwy 33 - N58 57 40 W002 54 18

| M 0 | 500 | 1000 |
| FT 0 | 1000 | 2000 | 3000 | 4000 |

RWY	SLOPE	LDA m/ft	APP LGT		RWY LGT
09(088°T)	0·02%D	1268/4160	P 3·5° (42)	❶CL5B	RTHL (H+WB);REDL (H:O);RENL
27(268°T)	0·02%U	1326/4350	P 3·5° (47)	CL2B	
15(140°T)	0·54%U	560/1837	-	-	-
33(320°T)	0·54%D	560/1837	-	-	-

❶ App lgt CL5B: 900m.
2. **Rwy 15/33.** HJ only. First part of Rwy 33 tarmac has steep down gradient (2%).
3. **Rwy 27.** Severe turb & and occasionally windsheer, may be encountered on short finals below 400ft during periods of strong winds from btn SW and NW.
4. **Rwy 27.** Hgt allowance of 15ft to be applied to performance calculations for dep due to vehicles on road under TKOF and climb paths for these rwys.
5. Other than the Eastern twy, which is avbl HJ by acft with an outer main gear wheel span less than 5m & wingspan less than 24m, no other twys are avbl for use by acft requiring a licensed AD
6. The Eastern twy is avbl HJ only.
7. Flying by acft not requiring a licensed AD may be permitted by the licensee & may occur at any time in daylight hours outside of published hours.
8. Security post 3m high at the apron edge adjacent to passenger gates. Pilots of acft not receiving marshalling assistance should exercise caution when taxiing or parking in front of the terminal.
9. Due to proximity to Shanwick Oceanic bdry pilots must consider timescales for requesting Oceanic clnc. Such clnc (inc lvl allocation) is valid only from OCA Entry Point, **domestic ATC clnc to this point is issued seperately.**

(Courtesy of European Aeronautical Group)

89

Sixty years ago

Sixty years ago, Ivy Cooper of Kirkwall became part of the exciting world of air travel. Writing in 2002, she recalled what it was like.

"I worked for the Airways from 1944 to 1953. As you'll realise, my recall is in the dim past, but I have some kind of remembrance which might be of interest. If not, no matter!

"Captain Fresson's *Air Road to the Isles* will have accurate dates, etc., but I think it was Highland Airways I joined in 1944 at a weekly wage of fifteen shillings, which eventually rose to One Pound. Then it was called Scottish Airways which operated the Kirkwall-Inverness route, whereas Mr Gandar Dower's service, Allied Airways, worked the Kirkwall-Aberdeen line. When I joined BEA, I earned £2 12s a week, riches indeed.

"Passengers arrived and left from the office in Broad Street, as the aerodrome would be a restricted area and passengers and their baggage were weighed in the office. There was a secret sign on the booking list highlighting a 'heavy-weight'. Every morning, the Army Traffic Control Officer for the aerodrome arrived for the list of passengers. Much to his embarrassment one morning, I listed a soldier as 'Bdr', which he interpreted as 'bombardier'. So he was taken aback when a brigadier stood at his desk.

"There would be only eight seats on each flight, so there was always a waiting list. As it was anticipated that there might be priority bookings, a couple of seats were kept open to avoid displacement. So standby passengers are nothing new. To book a return seat, a teleprinter message was sent to Inverness in code. All I can remember was the first, ABAZ, which I think meant 'Book one seat Inverness-Kirkwall, the date, time and name of passenger.

"One of the Inverness staff had a sister stationed in Kirkwall in the WRNS, so there was a special arrangement for their mail to be 'posted' on the planes. On one occasion, she needed some clean collars urgently, so a message was sent: 'ABAZ Inverness-Kirkwall, the date, Sybil Clean Collars'. It worked! Rather than endure the Pentland Firth steamer crossing and long train journey, many service personnel saved up to fly home for their leave, and they got a fare reduction.

"A little freight was carried. On one occasion, Captain Fresson (I think he was affectionately known as 'Uncle' by the staff) had agreed to take a bouquet of flowers to a friend in Bettyhill. The plan was to throw them out of the plane as he flew over. Alas it got caught under the plane, so no flowers. A farmer in Tankerness arranged for day-old chickens to be taken up by air. They arrived in flat-holed cardboard boxes. I can still mind their 'cheep-cheep' as they waited to be picked up. When one of the Orkney ministers was appointed Moderator of the Church of Scotland, very special lace was required for his moderator's jacket. So how to get this precious cargo to Edinburgh? Enquiries were made to see if there was a trustworthy passenger booked who could be the messenger. Problem soon solved for there was a weel-kent Sunday School teacher booked on just the right day!"

C.

BRITISH EUROPEAN AIRWAYS CORPORATION

SCOTTISH DIVISION,
AIRPORT FOR GLASGOW,
RENFREW.

TELEGRAMS : BEALINE Renfrew.

TELEPHONE : RENFREW 2231.

Miss I.A. Cooper,
Burnarvie House,
Junction Road,
Kirkwall.
Dear Madam,

February, 1947.

1. British European Airways Corporation (hereinafter referred to as "B.E.A.") has pleasure in offering you employment on the following terms :—

Occupation   Clerkess   Salary Scale   Age
Salary payable will be £2:12:-d   per week, rising, subject to satisfactory service, by annual increments of .... per week to .... per week, the maximum of the Salary Scale.

Acceptance of this offer will be deemed proof of your willingness to be employed by B.E.A. at any B.E.A. Station or Base at home or abroad.

All appointments are in the first instance for a probationary period of six months from the date of commencing employment. Subject to there being vacancies on the Established Staff and to a satisfactory report you will be eligible for inclusion on the Established Staff of B.E.A.

2. Your date of engagement is 1st August, 1946. Your base on engagement is Kirkwall   reporting to Station Superintendent.

3. The engagement is subject to references being satisfactory to B.E.A. and can be terminated by seven days' written notice on either side.

4. All employment is subject to the Orders and Instructions published by B.E.A. as amended from time to time. Staff are deemed to be aware of the contents of all Orders and Instructions applicable to their employment. As soon as practicable all members of the staff should ask their Branch or Departmental head to make such Orders and Instructions available for inspection.

5. It will be necessary for you to satisfy B.E.A. Medical Branch as to your fitness to perform the above duties, and you will receive instructions regarding Medical examination.

6. It is a condition of this engagement that you are accepted by the Guarantee Society. An application form is enclosed with this letter which should be completed and returned to this office. The premium on this insurance is payable by B.E.A.

7. Please indicate your acceptance of this appointment by signing the Declaration on the reverse of the top copy of this letter, then detach and return to the above address. The second copy of this letter should be retained by you for reference.

Yours faithfully,

A. C. PHILLIPS,
Staff Superintendent, Scottish Division.
For and on behalf of
BRITISH EUROPEAN AIRWAYS CORPORATION.

(courtesy of Ivy Cooper)

91

Air mail – First Day Covers

From the beginning of his first regular air services, Ted Fresson spotted the publicity value afforded by the carriage of specially designed first day covers. It is a tradition for marking special events that has endured.

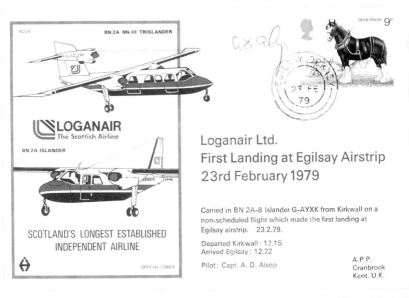

Loganair Ltd.
First Landing at Egilsay Airstrip
23rd February 1979

Carried in BN 2A-8 Islander G-AYXK from Kirkwall on a non-scheduled flight which made the first landing at Egilsay airstrip.   23.2.79.

Departed Kirkwall : 12.15
Arrived Egilsay : 12.22

A.P.P.
Pilot : Capt. A. D. Alsop   Cranbrook
Kent, U.K.

(courtesy of Loganair, Kirkwall)

BRITISH AIRWAYS

St. Magnus Cathedral
1137 - 1987

Inaugural Flight
1987
Kirkwall - Bergen

CARRIED ON BOARD

HS748 - St. Magnus of Orkney
Flight BA982 - 5th June 1987
AIRCRAFT COMMANDER

(courtesy of Janette Ridgway)

(Iain Hutchison Collection)

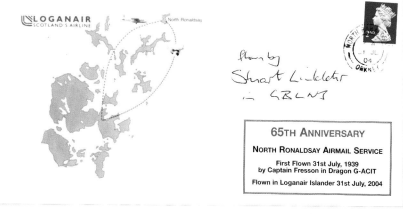

(Iain Hutchison Collection)

Bibliography

Barnes, Fred, 'Highland Budgies', *Propliner*, 100, Autumn 2004.

Clegg, Peter V, *Flying Against the Elements*, (Godalming: Peter Clegg, 1987)

Clegg, Peter V, *Sword in the Sky*, (Godalming: Peter Clegg, 1990)

Clegg, Peter V, *Wings over the Glens*, (Peterborough: GMS Enterprises, 1995)

Fresson, Captain E E, *Air Road to the Isles*, (London: David Rendel Ltd, 1967)

Gillies, J D, and Wood, J L, *Aviation in Scotland*, (Glasgow: Royal Aeronautical Society, 1966)

Helmsdal, Mikkjal, *Landsverkfrøđingsstovnurin 50 ár'*, (Tórshavn: Landsverkfrøđingurin, 1998)

Hutchison, Iain, *The Story of Loganair*, (Stornoway: Western Isles Publishing Co Ltd, 1987)

Hutchison, Iain, *The Flight of the Starling*, (Erskine: Kea Publishing, 1992)

Hutchison, Iain, *Air Ambulance*, (Erskine: Kea Publishing, 1996)

Lo Bao, Phil, *An Illustrated History of British European Airways*, (Feltham: Browcom Group plc, 1989)

Lo Bao, Phil, and Iain Hutchison, *BEAline to the Islands*, (Erskine: Kea Publishing, 2002)

McIlroy, John, 'The extrovert pilot whose charm touched Orkney', *Orkney Today*, 19 December 2003

Partner, David, *People and Places*, (Kirkwall: The Orcadian Ltd, 2001)

Scott, Jack, *Wings over Westray*, (Finstown: InformationPlus, 1997)

Sinclair, Norman, *Images in Time, Volumes 1 and 3*, (Kirkwall: The Orcadian Ltd, 2001)

Stroud, John, *Railway Air Services*, (Shepperton: Ian Allan Ltd, 1987)

Other sources

Herald Facts 39 (Cricklewood: Handley Page Ltd, 1964)

Highland Airways Orkney and Shetland brochure (Inverness: Highland Airways, 1937)

Loganair news cutting collection, Kirkwall Airport

The Orcadian newspaper

Acknowledgements

Grateful thanks are due to Iain Hutchison for his always helpful advice, his hard work, his patience, editorial and creative skills; to James Miller and Eileen Russell of *The Orcadian*; Robert Leslie at Kirkwall Public Library, Elaine Scott, Neil Thain and Michael Firth at Kirkwall Airport; Christine Allan, Ivor Robertson, Stuart Linklater, Stephen Gates and Ian Potten of Loganair; Robert Milne of British Airways, Kirkwall; Basil O'Fee of Highland Airways; Morag Robertson at Orkney Islands Council. Also to Andy and Glenys Alsop; Peter Amos of the Miles Aircraft Collection; Nat Anderson of Highlands & Islands Airports Ltd; Ken Best; Michael Bradshaw; Ian Brown of the Museum of Flight, East Fortune; Andy Clancey and Allan Wright of B-N Historians; Peter V Clegg; Ivy Cooper; David Earl; Ken Ebsworth and Harry Fraser-Mitchell of the Handley Page Association; Robert Foden; Keith Hayward, British Airways archivist; Philip Jarrett; Brian Kemp; Björn Larsson; John McDonald; Moya McDonald; Lesley McLetchie; Paul McMaster; David Partner; Anker Eli Petersen; David Rendall; Janette Ridgway; Norman Sinclair; Nick Stroud; Ray Sturtivant; and Tommy Tullock. The author is particularly grateful to Orkney Libraries for granting permission for reproduction from its photographic archive of many of the period images in this book, and to David Mackie for his invaluable technical advice.

Strenuous efforts have been made to verify the originators of photographic material and to contact them for their permission to reproduce their work. Sincere apologies are extended to anyone who feels that they have been omitted from the normal courtesies for seeking the reproduction of material.

A special word of thanks goes to Jane Glue who created the painting for the front cover, and to Debbie Low of *The Kirkwall Hotel* for sponsoring Jane's work. The support of Scott Grier, Chairman of Loganair, and his contribution of the foreword, are greatly appreciated. Acknowledgement and thanks are also expressed to the Economic Development Service of the Orkney Islands Council which kindly granted funding towards the publication of this book.

Last, but by no means least, a very special thanks must go to my wife, Lynda, for all her support, constructive advice and coffee.

The publisher extends additional thanks to Roger Carvell; David Doak; David Dyer; Douglas Nicolson; and Wallace Shackleton for their help.

Flying People
- bringing you safe flying, every day

by
Graham Perry

Flying People is a wry look at the last fifty years of a century of flying, and especially at the character and determination of the people who, during that time, have made it a safe, everyday event. Because flying could so easily end in tears, it is a serious business – and aviation's people have developed their own ways of dealing with its many challenges. Perry demonstrates that they are problem-solvers, they are conscientious, they think and work as a team, and they readily share the lessons from their mistakes. Most of all, they dispense a cheerful cynicism as they defeat anyone and anything that threatens safe flying. Flying people have brought about safe, affordable ways of flying the world's people everywhere. This book celebrates them all.

Described by one commercial pilot as "having something for air travellers, aviation enthusiasts and professional pilots", he assesses *Flying People* as "an excellent read, well written and very informative." *Flying People* has been illustrated by *figment*, the nom-de-plume of John Reed, celebrated contributing artist to the journal of the British Air Line Pilots Association.

"Perry writes with a twinkle in his eye and he takes a serious subject and exposes the fun to be had." *Air Cadet*

"Anyone who has been involved in aviation will thoroughly enjoy this book and will recognise their own experiences. But with its clear explanations and easy-to-read style, it should also appeal to anyone who wants to understand the complicated world of aviation" *The Aerospace Professional*

Flying People
by Graham Perry
152 pages, over 20 illustrations
Softback. Cover price £12.95. ISBN 0 9518958 6 9

Available from:
Kea Publishing, 14 Flures Crescent, Erskine, Renfrewshire PA8 7DJ, Scotland.
Please add 10% for postage and packing; 25% for air mail outside Europe.
www.keapublishing.com

Whatever were you thinking of, Captain?

A Handbook for Airline Passengers

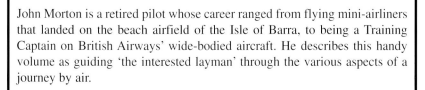

by

Captain John L. Morton

John Morton is a retired pilot whose career ranged from flying mini-airliners that landed on the beach airfield of the Isle of Barra, to being a Training Captain on British Airways' wide-bodied aircraft. He describes this handy volume as guiding 'the interested layman' through the various aspects of a journey by air.

While this book describes some of the technical aspects of an air journey, jargon is minimised and the practical aspect of the content is lightened with anecdote and humour. Its ultimate objective is intended to suggest a relaxed and confident atmosphere to flying.

Whatever were you thinking of, Captain? is illustrated by the artistic pen of *figment*, the nom-de-plume of John Reed, who is a long-time flight deck colleague of Morton.

Hailed as "…a mini-masterpiece" by the journal of the British Air Line Pilots Association, *The Log*.

Whatever were you thinking of, Captain?
by Captain John L. Morton
80 pages, 20 drawings, 4 maps and diagrams
Softback. Cover price £8.95. ISBN 0 9518958 5 0

Available from:
Kea Publishing, 14 Flures Crescent, Erskine, Renfrewshire PA8 7DJ, Scotland.
Please add 10% for postage and packing; 25% for air mail outside Europe.

www.keapublishing.com

BEAline to the Islands

The story of air services to offshore communities of the British Isles by British European Airways, its predecessors and successors

by
Phil Lo Bao and Iain Hutchison

For a quarter of a century, British European Airways Corporation operated an extensive network of air services to Europe and the Near East. Its services were patronised by those who were beneficiaries of the growing affluence which followed World War Two. However, for many people, air travel remained a luxury beyond their grasp and the airline, which claimed to be 'Foremost in Europe', had an elitist appeal to the travellers of the 1950s and 1960s.

Yet there was another BEA. This was the BEA which provided lifeline services to island communities around the British Isles. The airline's relationship with islanders was sometimes a turbulent one but these air links were jealously guarded. BEA's Rapides and Pionairs provided utilitarian flying but it was 'real' flying. *BEAline to the Islands* records the story of this other BEA.

"A welcome addition to the shelves as it covers an unsung, but essential, service to the far-flung islands." *Wingspan International*

"Whether you have enjoyed, or endured, flying to and from the isles, you'll find this a good read." *The Orcadian*

BEAline to the Islands
by Phil Lo Bao and Iain Hutchison
178 pages, 90 photographs, 5 maps
Softback. Cover price £14.95. ISBN 0 9518958 4 2

Available from:
Kea Publishing, 14 Flures Crescent, Erskine, Renfrewshire PA8 7DJ, Scotland.
Please add 10% for postage and packing; 25% for air mail outside Europe.

www.keapublishing.com

Times subject to Tides

The Story of Barra Airport

by

Roy Calderwood

Once remote and isolated, this all changed when the first aircraft to land on Barra arrived in 1933. The rocky terrain of the island meant that this aircraft had to land on a large expanse of beach called the Tràigh Mhòr. Aircraft still land on the beach at Barra although its air services have not been without controversy in recent years.

Times subject to Tides tells the story of this unique airport which disappears, under the sea, twice every day. It looks at the aircraft which have graced the broad sands of the Tràigh Mhòr, the personalities whose names have become indelibly linked with the island's air services, and at some of the drama which has inevitably become an accepted feature on certain occasions - not least of which are emergency air ambulance evacuations of seriously ill or injured islanders, or aircraft beleaguered in soft sand in the face of an advancing tide.

Roy Calderwood, who has been visiting Barra for many years, and whose manuscript began as a presentation folder compiled with no other objective than to entertain the airport's handful of staff, has compiled a fascinating story about a unique airport. And he has sourced the personal experiences of airline crews who cut their flying teeth on Herons to Barra – one went on to command Concorde.

"In the Foreword, Dr Winifred Ewing says, 'Landing by air on its cockle strand is one of the best air experiences in Europe. The sense of clean air and space is like heady wine.' This sums up the book admirably." *Air Pictorial*

"To those, such as myself, who were lucky enough to have spent time flying to Barra and the other islands in the past, this book will bring back a host of memories." Captain Peter Morgan writing in *The Log*

Times subject to Tides
by Roy Calderwood
112 pages, 42 photographs, 4 maps
Softback. Cover price £9.95. ISBN 0 9518958 3 4

Available from:
Kea Publishing, 14 Flures Crescent, Erskine, Renfrewshire PA8 7DJ, Scotland.
Please add 10% for postage and packing; 25% for air mail outside Europe.

www.keapublishing.com

Air Ambulance

Sixty years of the Scottish Air Ambulance Service

by *Iain Hutchison*

The Scottish Air Ambulance Service came into being on 14 May 1933 when John McDermid, a fisherman on the Isle of Islay, was uplifted by a de Havilland Dragon aircraft of Midland & Scottish Air Ferries. Piloted by Jimmy Orrell, the aircraft had been requested by Dr Stewart for his thirty-three year old patient who had a perforation of the stomach carrying the risk of peritonitis. Orrell made a beach landing at Bridgend to collect McDermid who was speedily transported to Renfrew Aerodrome and onwards to Glasgow's Western Infirmary where he was soon removed from danger.

Today, the Scottish Air Ambulance Service is a vital component of the country's healthcare services, utilizing both fixed-wing aircraft and helicopters. A book of two parts, it tells 'The Air Ambulance Story' of how the service developed during its first sixty years. In the second part, it relates 'The Air Ambulance Experience,' which includes personal accounts of pilots and airline personnel, doctors and nurses, and, of course, patients, during from those sixty years.

Maternity cases were to become a regular part of the work of the Service. However, not all expectant mothers made it to the delivery room on time, and *Air Ambulance* lists a unique group of babies who were 'born on a plane'.

"This book should be read by all those who regard the aeroplane as a means of enhancing and improving our way of life, rather than as a means of destroying it. I compliment Iain for his diligence in fulfilling a heartfelt need, thank him for enriching the annals of aviation experience, and paying tribute to the exploits and achievements of the wonderful men and women of the Scottish Air Ambulance Service whose light has hitherto been hidden under the proverbial bushel." *R E G Davies FRAeS FRSA, Curator of Air Transport, National Air and Space Museum, Smithsonian Institution, Washington DC.*

"…crammed with great human stories of courage and resilience, flying prowess and sheer heroism." *James Henderson, The Northern Times*

Air Ambulance
by Iain Hutchison
192 pages, 62 photographs, 6 maps
Hardback. Cover price £19.95. ISBN 0 9518958 2 6
Available from:
Kea Publishing, 14 Flures Crescent, Erskine, Renfrewshire PA8 7DJ, Scotland.
Please add 10% for postage and packing; 25% for air mail outside Europe.

www.keapublishing.com

The story of Loganair

Scotland's Airline – the first 25 years

by
Iain Hutchison

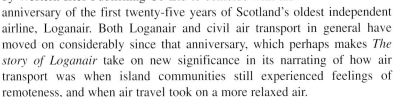

This was Iain Hutchison's first book and it was published by Western Isles Publishing Co Ltd to coincide with the anniversary of the first twenty-five years of Scotland's oldest independent airline, Loganair. Both Loganair and civil air transport in general have moved on considerably since that anniversary, which perhaps makes *The story of Loganair* take on new significance in its narrating of how air transport was when island communities still experienced feelings of remoteness, and when air travel took on a more relaxed air.

When Loganair began as an air taxi operator in 1962, Scotland's scheduled air services were religiously guarded by the state-owned airline British European Airways. However, Loganair gradually found a role in the country lanes of Scotland's skies, bringing air services to locations that BEA could not serve. Loganair developed new airfields, much as the pioneers of the 1930s had done, and it undertook air ambulance flights in 1967, assuming full responsibility for the Scottish Air Ambulance Service in 1973. In 1969 it began its first international scheduled services – to Norway, and by 1987 it served twenty-nine UK airports, more than any other airline.

Kea Publishing acquired *The story of Loganair* when the proprietor of Western Isles Publishing took a well-earned retirement.

"A most readable book, well produced and one of the most useful volumes to cross my desk for some time past." *J.D. Ferguson, Aviation News*

The story of Loganair
by Iain Hutchison
96 pages, 52 photographs, 12 maps
Softback. Cover price £4.95. ISBN 0 906437 14 8
Available from:
Kea Publishing, 14 Flures Crescent, Erskine, Renfrewshire PA8 7DJ, Scotland.
Please add 10% for postage and packing; 25% for air mail outside Europe.
www.keapublishing.com

Index